Religion and Change in Contemporary Asia

Published with assistance from
the Roger E. Joseph Memorial Fund
for greater understanding
of public affairs, a cause in which
Roger Joseph believed

Religion
and Change
in Contemporary
Asia

Edited by ROBERT F. SPENCER

University of Minnesota Press   Minneapolis

Library of Congress Catalog Card Number: 76-139450

ISBN 0-8166-0610-2

Preface

The essays in this volume arise from a series of lectures on the general topic of religion and contemporary affairs in Asia. These lectures were presented on the Minneapolis campus of the University of Minnesota in the spring of 1968. They were sponsored by the All-University Committee on Asia with the support, here gratefully acknowledged, of the university's Office of International Programs and its dean, Willard W. Cochrane.

Students of area studies in general and particularly those with Asian interests have for some time been confronted with the need to find a common level of discourse. The several specific disciplines in the social sciences and humanities come to the long history and the complex societies of Asia with somewhat different points of view. They frequently find it difficult to locate a prevailing emphasis which can serve to put developments in Asia into sharper focus. The general topic selected here — religion in Asia — seems, however, well suited to effect a meeting ground of several disciplines. The contributors are well-known scholars in fields relating to Asian studies; each has engaged in long-term and careful research in the area which he discusses.

R. F. S.

v

Contents

Religion and Change in Contemporary Asia

⟩ ROBERT F. SPENCER ⟨

Introduction · Religion in Asian Society

IT IS obvious that coverage of the entire range of Asian problems
as they relate to religion is impossible within the compass of this
volume. Enough is suggested in the following essays, however, to
convey some sense of the place of religion in the differing Asian
cultures, its function in promoting or hindering change, and its
continuing role in the promotion of societal stability. The emphasis of these essays is on the contemporary, an aspect which at
once suggests the element of the political, for religion has come today to serve as a handmaiden for nationalism and nationalist as-
piration. Some of the papers which follow stress this side of religious development. Nations in turmoil, such as Vietnam, Indonesia, or even China, may be obliged to discover new applications
of the past in order to face the present. Others, such as Japan and
Pakistan, may find through religion a partial solution to the problem of democratization versus authoritarianism. But politics is
not the whole story, since still other countries, notably India and
Burma, appear generally to separate the religious from the political, locating a continuing source of inspiration in the traditional.
There are in short any number of answers to the questions raised

3

about the part religion plays in Asian or for that matter in any society.

The general topic of religion and contemporary affairs can be approached from several different points of view. There are always in a volume of this kind some vexing problems of definition. These relate first of all to the Asian land mass itself, for in terms of religious content there is really little in common between Islam and Confucianism, or indeed between the Buddhism of the Theravada and Mahayanist persuasions. But at a more fundamental level there is also the question of precisely what religion is. The line of thought which has traditionally taken the concept *religion* as a panhuman phenomenon, separating it from other social institutions or examining it in its philosophical, historical, and humanistic contexts, has been of late undergoing some rather radical revision. A great deal is already known of the history and nature of the religions of Asia; now, as the construct *religion* is rethought, is it possible to say something more about its place in the Asian sphere or in human experience anywhere?

In the vast land mass of Asia are to be found the origins of the great civilizations of mankind. The Near East, India, and China were heartlands, foci, where through varying circumstances and accidents of history lasting and distinctive traditions came into being. These "great traditions" spread from their centers of origin to influence adjacent areas. Japan and Korea, for example, along with what has today become Vietnam, were drawn into the sphere of Chinese civilization, while the rich culture of India made its mark on Southeast Asia and Indonesia. Islam, originating in the Near East, left its imprint variously on the peoples of South Asia. Along with the inventions, technological and social, which each center provided, and interwoven intimately and intricately with them, are systems of ideas, perceptions of man and the world, of the human fate and condition, which are generally credited as reflecting the religious institutions. Deeply rooted in time and yet subject to change in both spatial and temporal terms, the religions of Asia have come virtually to stand for Asian society, at least to the secularized Western mind.

It is true that these great traditions reflect specific kinds of orientations, ways of looking at the world, and situational definitions which provide a yardstick against which to measure human reaction and behavior.

But there nevertheless remains the difficulty of defining religion. It is considerably more than belief and ritualistic action. It consists of a series of propositions, often only implicit, about the nature of reality. Religion has been traditionally thought of as a means of coping with life; to find in religion a way of conceiving it is to suggest some different insights (Geertz, 1968, p. 93).

There can be no question that religion in its wider sense has been a vital part of the organization of the various Asian socio-cultural systems. But the contributors to this symposium are agreed that religion need not be the only key to the understanding of the various Asian peoples, a point especially true today when it is noted that the various cultural groupings of Asia have become nations and been obliged to take a position vis-à-vis the West in economic, political, and international affairs. A process of acculturation has been operative, meaning that the Asians have been forced into the Westernized mold of nation with all the legalistic, organizational, economic, industrial, and military adaptations that this implies. In many instances, this has demanded a high price, especially since modernism, in the sense of Westernization, either conflicts with tradition or requires the reorganization of traditional patterns of thought, belief, and behavior. Add to this the problems of demography and poverty and the issues become complex indeed. Some Asian nations are clearly more successful in achieving a balance between the traditional and the new, a point which can be amply demonstrated when the religious systems in each area are compared. In other words, giving special thought to the experience of the Asian peoples, it is in religion that a fuller understanding of the nature of changing patterns can lie. For in fact if religion seen in its broadest sense offers an approach to reality — at least to the way in which reality is perceived by the various cultural systems developing in Asia — then the processes of change

5

must operate within the framework supplied by such conceptions of reality.

It is thus not sufficient to treat religion as an isolate. It is rather to be seen as a human institution and as a mode of thought as well, both arising within a socio-cultural matrix. Men in society act and behave because of what appears to them as a series of self-evident truths. On the level of the more elaborated civilizations — those societies and cultures which have developed bodies of tradition perpetuated through writing — there is the development of a concept of history, in itself a self-evident truth, which gives meaning to tradition and which determines the ordering of change. Sometimes the concept of history relates to an actual historical time and sometimes not. The point may be made that whether the historic process is seen as fact or as myth it still reflects a conceptual truth which governs human action and which possesses a character of the sacred. Primitive religions, in fact, as distinct from the great traditions of what are conventionally designated as civilizations, tend to lack the historical dimension even if timeless myth may provide a rationale for behavior.

It is fairly easy to exemplify the point. To name one culture, or rather, one major civilization, it can be said that India has never been oriented toward historic time, a development which can be fairly readily understood when the other-worldly quality of the Indian ethos is considered. But on the other hand, there is the element of myth as history, meaning that whether the concern is for the Buddha, the god Vishnu, the *Purānas*, or whatever, the element of the myth comes to have the force of history and so to some degree to govern, if not events directly, at least the behavioral associations which precipitate events. A parallel of a quite different order can be seen in China and in the areas influenced by Chinese civilization, where history is used to buttress a concept of morality, and where there is little primary concern for the ostensible accuracy of the historic record (cf. Smith, 1966, p. 19).

The way in which a people approaches its own sense of its past is a reflection of its culturally derived view of reality and of the sacred. Every religious system, in a synchronic sense, is an end

6

product which consists of a totality of rituals, symbols, and elements of value. This is the overt side of religion, the component elements which can be seen. But there is the other side as well, one resident in the mood that is created by religious acts, the feeling tone or atmosphere reflecting a specialized commitment. This is a total ethic, an "ethos," a set of orientations which may begin in religion, especially among the Asian peoples, and then come to color the entire life style of a culture. To call a total social system "Magian," "Faustian," or Apollonian-Dionysian in the Nietzschean or Spenglerian sense is admittedly not very helpful. Yet here is one fairly simplistic way of attempting to come to grips with the specialized commitment of various civilizations. And it is necessary to attempt to deal with the problem. This is especially true in Asia, where any item, however commonplace in the West, a television set, say, or a bulldozer, is appraised in line with a different perception of the world and so develops around itself a different set of associations. All of the contributors to the present volume have been obliged to take this issue into account, handling it either directly or implicitly. The formal and observable aspects of religion in Asia, or indeed in the West, can be readily described; it is the covert aspect, the mood, the atmosphere, the essentially hidden dimension which require exposition (Geertz, 1958).

Thus when a Chinese, in the classical sense, defines human social and political roles as part of an inflexible natural order, as the Confucian dialectic prescribes, or when the Theravada Buddhist in Burma or Cambodia, Thailand or Ceylon, holds life to be impermanent and fraught with suffering, and consciousness a delusion, a spirit is created which pervades the behavioral systems of these respective peoples. It is probably true that no Hindu can make an absolute commitment to the notion that life and objective reality are illusory, however much he may be committed to philosophical Vedanta, yet at the same time his thought and behavior are influenced by it. To take another example, Christianity and Islam possess common historical roots. They share the same god, have basically the same eschatology, and are both committed to a rigorous and literal historicism. Yet neither in the modern

7

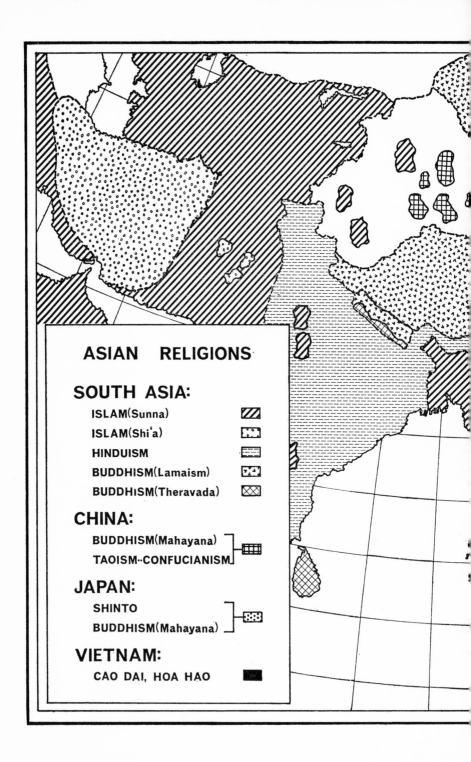

ASIAN RELIGIONS

SOUTH ASIA:
ISLAM(Sunna)
ISLAM(Shi'a)
HINDUISM
BUDDHISM(Lamaism)
BUDDHISM(Theravada)

CHINA:
BUDDHISM(Mahayana)
TAOISM--CONFUCIANISM

JAPAN:
SHINTO
BUDDHISM(Mahayana)

VIETNAM:
CAO DAI, HOA HAO

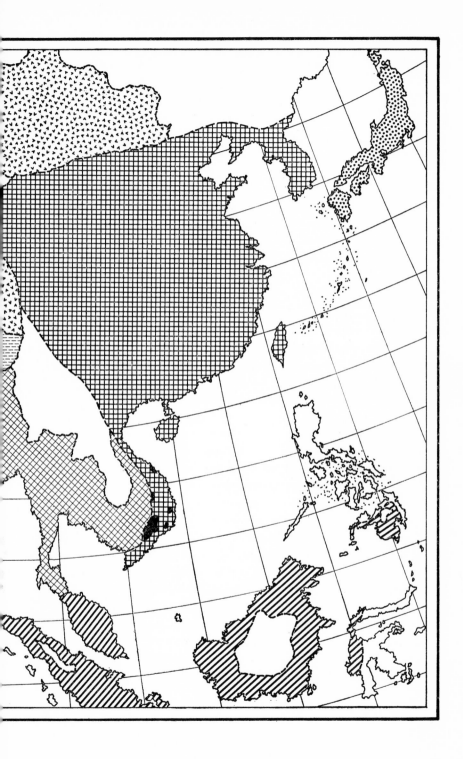

world nor in the past can they ever be said to have been alike. Man's approach to God in Islam is clearly of a different nature and order than is true in traditional Christianity.

What is involved is the "mood." If a culture may be defined as the sum totality of self-evident truths and values held by a people, these are in turn given direction and meaning through the avenue of the supernatural and the mystic, in other words, through religion. The lasting "mood" which Geertz finds essential to the definition of religion serves both to define the nature of the religious system and to reflect the character of the total cultural system as well (Geertz, 1966, p. 35–40). Geertz is of course saying something slightly different from a formulation which identifies a total ethic with a religious system. His "mood" is one in which the nature of reality as perceived by a given human group receives its channeling.

There are, of course, other ways of looking at religious issues. Religion is also a social institution and can be analyzed like any other institutional component in a society. But such a mode of analysis, whether basically psychological or sociological, assumes that the tenets of a religious system are untrue and unreal, an inevitable corollary of a perspective on religion which is ostensibly objective and presumably scientific. A serious injustice is done religious phenomena by such an approach, since it can never take into account precisely what it is that the "true believer" sees when he deals with the supernatural. It can probably be agreed that some element of supernaturalism is a basic prerequisite to any religious system in the narrower or institutional sense. Thus the Hindu who sees the world of phenomena as illusory, who possesses an essentially atheistic orientation, finding his reality in an impersonal cosmic All, may still perform rituals in order to avert misfortune. Parallels to this kind of behavioral situation are seen everywhere and it is here where the distinction between religion and magic, the other-worldly and the this-worldly concern, becomes hard to separate (Spiro, 1966, p. 94–97).

When religion is seen as a social institution, a structure-functional analysis tends to assume that the religious institutions may serve as a focus for the total society and may become the primary factors of unification or cohesion. Human societies may vary in respect to the institution which appears to become the primary element of organization and integration. In one, it may be the element of subsistence, in another the family, in a third religion. But especially in Asia, where the religious traditions prove so strong, it is not unexpected that the religious development should have more than casual importance. The traditional bases of religion often appear to be translated into the modern concepts of nationalism and to form the rationale for the existence of the nation-state. Pakistan, to name one, makes much of its Islamic tradition as the source of its nationhood, while the Theravada Buddhism of Burma apparently underlies not only the societal cohesion within the Burmese village but also the fierce sense of independence characteristic of the Burmese Union. The religious institutions cannot always be identified as primary forces of socio-cultural integration but they may interact with other social institutions so as to create the patterned solidarity of the societal entity. Thus in China religion lends meaning to the institutions of familism, even though Chinese culture itself is often described as lacking in god-mindedness. Such a statement about Chinese culture does not imply a detraction of Chinese religiosity, as Professor Wright notes, but arises from the fact that there are institutions among the Chinese where the emphasis is not religious.

These features — ethos, mood, society, social structure — are all in one way or another implicit in the essays which follow. In them the attempt is made to come to grips with the problems of religion, society, politics, and change in Asia. Given the ideal systems which intertwine with the great religions, with Islam, with Hinduism and Buddhism, Confucianism, Taoism, and Shinto, what have the various Asian peoples done to adapt themselves to the challenge of modern nationalism and all that it implies, as against the basic viewpoints which have come to them through time?

The arrangement of the studies which follow has been made with some thought toward the major cultural foci of Asia. They begin with China, where a major civilization has been caught in the dilemma of an artificial renascence. Japan and Vietnam, both of which fall into the sphere of Chinese civilization, are then considered. India follows, with its cultural dependent, Burma, as a representative of Theravada Buddhism in Southeast Asia. In Pakistan and Indonesia there are the traditions of the Near East, the culture world of Islam. The general impact of Christianity has been omitted in these essays. Judaeo-Christianity, to be sure, cannot be overlooked, especially on the modern scene. Yet it is perhaps this part of the total Western ethic which the Asians have found most difficult to assimilate. Despite the not inconsiderable impact made in the past by Christian missionization, the modern Asian seems to rationalize the modifications which occur at the economic, political, and social levels in terms of the traditional and indigenous rather than in the context of an imported ideology. How this rationalization can occur, how the modern nations of Asia have responded to the call to wed the traditional with the modern give rise to the complex series of questions to which the writers of these essays have addressed themselves.

REFERENCES

Geertz, Clifford
  1958. "Ethos, Worldview, and the Analysis of Sacred Symbols." *Antioch Review*, 58: 421–37.
  1960. *The Religion of Java.* Glencoe, Ill.: Free Press.
  1966. "Religion as a Cultural System." In *Anthropological Approaches to the Study of Religion*, ed. M. Banton, pp. 1–46. Association of Social Anthropologists of the Commonwealth, Monograph 3. London: Tavistock Publications.
  1968. *Islam Observed: Religious Development in Morocco and Indonesia.* New Haven: Yale University Press.
Leach, E. R.
  1968. "Introduction." In *Dialectic in Practical Religion*, ed. E. R. Leach, pp. 1–6. Cambridge: Cambridge University Press.
von der Mehden, Fred R.
  1963. *Religion and Nationalism in Southeast Asia.* Madison: University of Wisconsin Press.
Smith, Donald E.
  1966. "The Political Implications of Asian Religions." In *South Asian Politics and Religion*, ed. Donald E. Smith, pp. 3–20. Princeton: Princeton University Press.
  1966. "Emerging Patterns of Religion and Politics." in *South Asian Politics and*

Religion, ed. Donald E. Smith, pp. 21–48. Princeton: Princeton University Press.

Spiro, Melford E.

1966. "Religion: Problems of Definition and Explanation." In *Anthropological Approaches to the Study of Religion,* ed. M. Banton, pp. 85–126. Association of Social Anthropologists of the Commonwealth, Monograph 3. London: Tavistock Publications.

Turner, Victor W.

1969. *The Ritual Process.* Chicago: Aldine.

᠌ ARTHUR F. WRIGHT ᠌

Buddhism in Modern and Contemporary China

THE STORY of Buddhism in modern and contemporary China is intelligible only if it is viewed as one element in the prolonged and desperate struggle of the Chinese people since 1900 to build a viable modern culture out of the ruins of their ancient civilization. The ancient order was one of phenomenal coherence and amazing recuperative powers. Its death agonies were prolonged, and the quest for a new culture was complicated by the residual power of ancient habits and ideas — a power they retained even when the total structure which made them meaningful had collapsed.

Buddhism is only one strand of the Chinese cultural heritage which the men of modern China drew upon in their effort to find a way out of national disintegration and despair. They also drew upon Confucianism and Taoism and upon the various traditions of the West that flooded in upon them. These men were not ivory-tower speculators; they were rather men driven by catastrophic events to find some workable formula of national salvation and cultural regeneration and to test that formula in practical action. Buddhism then may be seen as one ingredient of many successive

14

and competing formulas of national salvation, existing in more or less stable amalgams with elements from other traditions.

One can discern four principal ways in which Buddhism was thus used by the thinkers and programmers of modern China, and a review of them may be helpful in understanding the fate of Buddhism in the Communist state and society which have developed since 1949. Let me specify these four uses of Buddhism before turning to a discussion of each of them in turn:

1. The use of Buddhism as a possible state religion on the Western pattern of state churches.

2. The use of Buddhism as a source for a new lay ethic, a "social gospel" for modern China.

3. The use of Buddhism as a common bond that might unite the Chinese with other emergent peoples of Asia in dealing with their common problems.

4. The use of Buddhism as a native — nationalist — counterweight to the alien ideas from the West that seemed to carry all before them.

It occurred to many thoughtful Chinese in the first quarter of this century that the Western nations owed much of their seemingly invincible material power to their religious establishments. This argument was pressed by the Christian missionaries. China appeared to lack the common drives, the social cohesion, the spurs to progress that Christianity apparently provided in the Western nations. If this were true, the Chinese reasoned, then China might do well to adopt and propagate a state religion of its own. One proposal was that Confucianism be refurbished and modernized and put to this use. Another was that Buddhism could be made to serve. Across the sea Japan was moving rapidly to build a modern Western-style state, and Buddhism was — at least semi-officially — the acknowledged religion of the new nation. The Buddhists of China formed one of their first modern-type organizations in order to prevent the adoption of Confucianism as a state religion.

Several factors combined to prevent the adoption of Buddhism. One was the disillusionment with the West brought on by World War I. The various national Christian faiths had apparently been ineffectual in preventing fratricidal war, in stemming the impulse to self-destruction which had taken possession of Western man in those dreadful years. Did China then need a state religion after all? Second, the rise of states dominated by secular ideologies such as Marxism and fascism also argued that a state need not have a common religion to become strong and successful. Third, and most important, Buddhism itself was singularly ill adapted to serve as a state religion or as the basis of state ideology. Arnold Toynbee once remarked that the Mahayana form of Buddhism was a politically incompetent religion. Its history in China bears this out. It had not developed in China a political philosophy or the means of sanctioning and rationalizing power. This realm of thought and action had been largely left to Confucianism, and neither Buddhist clergy nor laity had developed the organization or the techniques to influence major political decisions. Buddhism — with its view of the present world as a split second in infinite time — had concentrated on the accumulation of individual merit, on the pursuit of ultimate salvation across many lives. Therefore its followers had made their peace with whatever secular power happened to prevail, and the Chinese state had consistently controlled and restricted Buddhism's spheres of religious thought and action. Buddhism's lack of political interests, of organization and militancy, combined with its long history of subordination to the state, account in large measure for the fate which has befallen Buddhism under Republican and Communist governments.

Turning to the second use of Buddhism in modern China, we find that many thoughtful Chinese were aware that the crumbling ethics of official Confucianism were inadaptable to the needs of a citizenry of a modern state. What was needed was a new ethic which would inspire a concern for the community and the nation and a heightened respect for the individual. And many felt that these elements could be discovered and redefined out of the Buddhist tradition. There were solid historical grounds on which this could be argued. Buddhism had, in its years of strength, introduced into China the first universalistic ethic; it had inspired and fostered community — not family — enterprises for the common

16

good: organized charity, hospitals, homes for the aged, free hostels for travelers, and so forth. The insistence of all Buddhist sects on the primary importance of the salvation of the individual had struck another nonfamilial note for the first time. Thus we find reformers of many types searching out these elements from the Buddhist tradition and recasting them as parts of one or another formula for national salvation. Nationwide organizations of lay Buddhists developed a host of charitable and public service operations. There were the new Western-style youth organizations, the YMBA and the YWBA; there were famine relief and war service organizations; and conferences on problems of religion, ethics, and social welfare. Efforts were made to activate home missionary enterprises to carry a modernized Buddhism to all parts of China; free books and pamphlets were distributed, itinerant preaching was carried on with some vigor. What, then, happened to these efforts to promote Buddhism as the lay ethic of a modernized China? Why did they fail?

One of the reasons for ultimate failure was the continuation of a social cleavage that went back many centuries in the history of Chinese Buddhism. The new movements attracted intellectuals, city dwellers, and the well-to-do of rural China. They did not succeed in reaching the mass of the peasantry, which continued to patronize an ancient folk religion compounded of native and Buddhist elements and perpetuated in the villages by ignorant and self-serving practitioners. The older Buddhist clergy, even when educated, were sunk in an immovable fatalism — a philosophical-emotional conviction that the "era of extinction of the faith" (*mo-fa*) had come. Nor would they abandon a life of monastic seclusion and the pursuit of salvation for active social and religious work among the laity. The handful of modern-minded militant clergy failed to move them, even as they failed to transform the superstitious cults of the peasant masses.

We find in the record other reasons for this failure. One was the persistently hostile attitude toward Buddhism of the various governments of the Republic. None of these governments — any more than the governments of imperial China — wanted a strong inde-

17

pendent church, and Buddhist temples and land were subjected to confiscation or discriminatory taxation. Thousands of temples and shrines were converted into barracks, police stations, or schools and their clergy forcibly secularized. As we have noted, the aftermath of World War I saw a great disillusionment in China with the religion of the West; there followed shortly a nationwide "anti-religious movement" in which religion was associated with backwardness, with the aggressions of the imperialist powers, with the violation of China's sovereign rights. Against all religious beliefs were set the claims of science.

The visit to China of the great Indian sage and poet Rabindranath Tagore in the 1920s redirected some of the nationalistic fire of the antireligionists from Christianity onto Hinduism and Buddhism. Tagore preached a lofty spirituality, tolerance, and compassion, and he appealed to the Chinese to revive their Buddhist faith. He was, however, attacked by the antireligionists as a living symbol of the "slave-religions" of India and China — religions which, they maintained, taught people to acquiesce in oppression and exploitation. All these inner difficulties and external pressures combined to constrain the spread of a modernized Buddhism, to restrict its influence and limit its impact. Nonetheless the movement for a modern Buddhism continued well into the period of the war against Japan; it is during this period, for reasons to be noted, that the movement begins to disintegrate.

The third use of Buddhism has been as an international, all-Asian, political cement, and in the end the attempt contributed greatly to its eclipse in China. The reason for this lay in the fact that the attempt was made, not by the Chinese, but by Japan as a stratagem in her pursuit of regional power in Eastern Asia. Japan had insisted on the right of Japanese Buddhist missionaries to reside in China and spread their faith there. This was a part of the infamous system of unequal treaties imposed on China by the Western powers and Japan which had guaranteed such rights for the Christian missionaries. With development of the idea of a Greater East Asia Co-Prosperity Sphere, Japan began to use Chinese Buddhists and Buddhist organizations to reduce resist-

ance among the Chinese. The Sino-Japanese organization known
as the *T'ung-yüan hui,* "Society of the Common Vow (to save living creatures)," was one among many that Japan sponsored.
When the Japanese came to control large areas of north and central China, they patronized Buddhism, rehabilitated temples, and
gave special favors to prominent Chinese Buddhists who would
cooperate with them. The public association of Buddhism with
collaborationism dealt the faith a serious blow in a time of heightened patriotic and national feeling. And it highlighted the fact that
Chinese Buddhism had not adapted itself to the rise of nationalism as Japanese Buddhism had managed to do. Chinese Buddhism
had remained cosmopolitan and thus was bound to suffer when
national feeling ran high in time of war. As we shall note later, such
cosmopolitanism had a certain usefulness to Chinese leaders when
they themselves were in a position to manipulate it. But the years
of war, 1937–45, saw Buddhism as a Chinese religion greatly weakened by the taint of collaborationism.

The fourth and final use of Buddhism in modern China has been
as an intellectual counterweight to the seemingly all-powerful
ideas which came from the West. No people with a long and proud
history of practical and intellectual achievement likes to acknowl-
edge that all native ideas are inferior to those imported from
abroad — to ideas developed by peoples who, only yesterday, were
regarded by the Chinese as contemptible barbarians. Confucianism had been so closely associated in every respect with the decay-
ing sociopolitical order of imperial China that it shared the oblo-
quy of the collapse of that order. Many Chinese, in a mood of cultural defensiveness, turned to the Buddhist tradition for ideas that
might be competitive with or possibly superior to those of the
modern West. Like other peoples of eastern and southern Asia, the
Chinese found that Buddhist metaphysicians had anticipated Ein-
steinian physics, that Buddhist organizations had been pioneers
in the application of the principles of equality and democracy to
group life, that Buddhist psychologists had been more perceptive
— and a millennium earlier — than Freud and Jung, and so on. To
a large extent the defensive apologetic tone of many of these claims

19

vitiated their effectiveness. Whatever truth there might be in them, it was never argued in a cool, logically consistent way but asserted with the force of emotional need.

Even as these claims were being made, they came under violent attack from radical modernizers whose ideal was "science" and whose thinking was, as the years went on, increasingly materialistic. Buddhism was associated in their minds not only with religion — which, they claimed, the West was discarding as outworn — but with metaphysics, with speculation rather than experiment and proof. Naturally such Chinese as Hu Shih found that certain strains in the Chinese intellectual tradition had been proto-scientific, and he and others like him argued that Buddhist metaphysics had rendered these trends abortive and deprived China of an indigenous science. Buddhism was thus made the scapegoat for China's intellectual backwardness.

The rising tide of materialist thought in China from 1920 onward seems to have been irresistible; and as it rose it slowly engulfed all forms of idealist philosophy whether Western or Buddhist. Kant and Hegel with their recent and shallow roots in China were swept away, along with varieties of Buddhist philosophy that had been introduced a millennium and a half earlier. This rising tide was not something observed and criticized from assorted ivory towers; it involved issues that were central to the controversy over the salvation and destiny of China. There were those who said that all nonmaterialist philosophies were on the decline in the West, headed for the discard in the very society that had produced them; like religion they were anachronisms in a world to be built and understood in terms of science. Those who would build a truly "modern" China should have nothing to do with such out-of-date nonsense. It was also argued that China's problems were basically material — a result of technological and industrial backwardness — and that therefore a philosophy which explained and prescribed for societies in material terms would be most directly applicable to China's problems. After 1917 Sun Yat-sen and other leaders watched the modernization of Russia under what appeared to be the materialist principles of Marxism. Nothing commends a system of thought like success-in-action, especially when, as in this case, the realm of application was a nation with problems similar to China's own.

Naturally this rising tide, these assorted arguments, did not go unchallenged. Many insisted that China needed most of all, and first of all, a thoroughgoing spiritual regeneration, a new ethic, a modern concept of the personality. But it should be noted that those who spoke in terms of such a priority were often the ones who clung with the greatest tenacity to ancient institutions and habits. The pseudo-Bergsonian vitalism of Chen Li-fu was a screen for one of the most reactionary and corrupt groups within the Kuomintang. The Nationalists' own "New Life Movement," seemingly based on the most lofty principles, was in fact an effort to retain as much as possible of the old society of status wherever and whenever it would make the public more docile and acquiescent in Nationalist rule. Buddhist idealisms — particularly as they became explicitly used to rationalize the Japanese militarist state — shared in the discredit and the negative criticism that came to be leveled against all idealisms. Far from being counterweights to Western intellectual dominance, they were held to be invalid, inapplicable, anachronistic, and all too convenient rationalizations of tyranny and oppression.

As the foregoing survey indicates, the efforts to use a modernized Buddhism as part of a new Chinese culture ended in failure. The failure was political, social, and intellectual. It is against this background that we must view the fate of Chinese Buddhism and Chinese Buddhists since the rise of Communist power. What has happened since 1949 has been in many respects a culmination of the trends perceivable in the preceding decades. It will be convenient to consider these recent developments under the general headings of political, social, and intellectual trends.

Political. The Communist constitution provides that "citizens of the People's Republic of China have freedom of religious belief." What this means in practice is similar to what it means in Russia. It also recalls the relation between the state and organized religion that prevailed in imperial China. It means that the state and the party allow people of various religious persuasions a limited and shrinking area of belief and action. The state and the party reserve the right to control all education, communication, and public and private morality. What autonomy is left to religious organizations or to the individual religious conscience is thus severely and strictly limited. If we note some of the measures of the Communist government, we can better understand what this supremacy of state and party over religion has meant in practice.

The secularization of Buddhist temples, lands, and clergy that had proceeded apace under the Kuomintang and warlord governments was pressed further. Buddhist temples and shrines numbered 268,000 in 1930, declined to about 130,000 in 1947, and were sharply reduced to less than 100 in 1954. The clergy may well have numbered 500,000 in 1931. By 1954 the number had been reduced to about 2,500. Temple lands were completely taken over by the state. The clergy who remained in the few operating temples had to find the means to sustain themselves — no easy task in a rigidly controlled economy. Many opened vegetarian restaurants, thus putting to public use the ancient recipes of the Chinese Buddhist cuisine. Parts of some temples were turned into handicraft factories or market gardens. Thus the ancient network of temples and shrines and of the clergy attached to them all but disappeared.

The state decreed that some of the ancient shrines were national monuments, "testimony to the creativity of the Chinese people despite their feudal oppressors." The cave temples of Tunhuang, Yunkang, Lungmen, and Mai-chi-shan as well as many old shrines in the cities were restored as cultural monuments. Thousands visit them every year, but they come not to worship some Buddha or Bodhisattva but, as the state insists, to glory in the perennial cultural creativity of the Chinese people. Some of these shrines and temples are preserved for another reason. Mao Tsetung has had political ambitions in Buddhist South and Southeast Asia. Visiting delegations of Buddhists from other countries were shown one of these serene, well-cared-for temples to demonstrate the Communist government's paternal concern for the Buddhist religion and for Buddhists everywhere. In this way Buddhism was manipulated by a Chinese government in the interest of its foreign policies. But even this limited showcase Buddhism has been adversely affected in the Cultural Revolution.

As we have seen, the modernizing Buddhists of China developed new organizations to defend and spread their faith. What happened to these further demonstrates the complete triumph of the state. The first nationwide organization of lay Buddhists was founded in 1914 to block the establishment of Confucianism as a state religion. Its successor was set up by the state in 1952 as one element in the network of organizations by which the state and party extended its control to every individual and household in China. The leadership was chosen by the party from among clergy and laymen who were deemed safe and docile. Their duties were to transmit the party's will to all Buddhists and to see to it that there was no deviation among Buddhists from the line laid down by the party. The tasks of Chinese Buddhists as laid down by a party leader in 1951 were the following: (1) participation in land reform, (2) opposition to counterrevolutionaries, (3) participation in the movement to resist America and aid Korea, and (4) recognition of the duty to construct a new religion in a new society. In short the new all-China association of Buddhists was to make sure that all Buddhists were active and disciplined subjects of the Communist state.

Social. We have seen that the modernizing Buddhists turned to social welfare work in the twentieth century. Today all the hospitals, homes for the aged, orphanages, and other similar institutions are run by the state and party. There is no sphere of private charity, and religion cannot claim the credit for ameliorating social ills. All such credit goes to the state and party. The debased folk Buddhism of the peasant masses, which the modern Buddhists had failed to reform, is now being systematically extirpated through anti-superstition and anti-illiteracy campaigns. It is being replaced not by a higher or a modernized religion, but by creeds, liturgies, and group activities sponsored by the party. The peasantry, in other words, are being converted directly from folk belief to the secular religion of Marxism-Leninism-Maoism.

The old dream of modern Buddhists that China might be regenerated through a new Buddhist ethic has likewise gone a-glimmering. The right to make ethical prescriptions for its subjects was consistently maintained by the rulers of imperial China. It is reasserted by the Communist government and enforced through an unprecedentedly thorough system of social and thought control. Party leaders decree what is good and proper conduct for the individual, and the network of party organs and state organizations propagates such standards among the populace. Chinese Communist ethics, a complex and fascinating amalgam of Western and Chinese elements, is the unchallenged ethical orthodoxy. Whenever the Buddhists make an ethical prescription, it must be reconciled with this orthodoxy. No deviation is permitted. This means in fact that Chinese Buddhism as an autonomous ethic is no more.

Intellectual. The multiple traditions of Chinese Buddhism provided a variety of philosophic ideas and of world views. As we have seen, many of these were revived and studied in the first four decades of this century. Today, however, the surviving thinkers who were once interested in these ideas have confessed the error of their ways. The total orthodoxy imposed by the state does not permit challenge or competition because Marxism-Leninism is held to be an all-encompassing and universal truth. The small seminaries and study groups founded by the Buddhists have been closed. All schools at all levels teach the official orthodoxy. Philosophical, historical, and other journals are all party-approved and party-operated. The two Buddhist monthlies allowed by the state preach total conformity to the party line; they have no intellectual distinctiveness or creativity, and their readership has dwindled to almost nothing, if indeed they are not now extinct. In this new society intellectual activity gains reward and recognition only when it serves the interests of state and party. As of the present, Chinese Buddhism is intellectually dead, and no new creative minds are being attracted to it.

As we reflect on the intellectual eclipse of this once-great philosophic tradition, we must recall the intellectual crisis and the intellectual needs of modern China. We have noted the seemingly irreversible tide of materialist thought, and we have speculated on the reasons for its success. But one further reason for the failure of Buddhism must be mentioned here. This is that its intellectual traditions are complex and varied, ranging from a logical-analytical strain to something like a pure intuitionism. No great intellectual leader emerged — though there were astute monk-politicians such as T'ai-hsü — to sort, sift, and organize a system of Buddhist thought adapted to the needs of modern China; intellectually Buddhism remained multiform and diffuse.

It would appear from the record that what modern Chinese man sought was a total coherent system that would analyze his individual and collective ills, prescribe for a new culture, and lay down rules for its further development. Neo-Confucianism had done this in the years of its strength. Marxism-Leninism claimed to do the same thing, and here we have an important reason for its steady rise long before the emergence of a Communist state. Buddhism offered no dream of an ideal society since, under its tenets, there could be no such society in a world of illusion and suffering. Buddhism did not deal in historical stages of social or economic development because such moments in infinite time were utterly insignificant. And despite the claims of its apologists, it did not have in it the germs of the scientific method. Marxism as total prescription and as pseudoscience has now achieved authority over the minds of the Chinese and has eliminated Buddhism from the spectrum of intellectual choice. The modifications which the Chinese have made and are likely to make in the Marxist intellectual system come not from the Buddhist heritage, but from the remnants of China's own secular philosophic tradition of Confucianism.

There are some lessons, some possibly general conclusions, that may be drawn from this somber picture of the twilight of a great religion in a culture it once deeply affected. One is to emphasize the general statement made earlier that Buddhism is a politically incompetent religion. It would take a great reformulator, an inspiring prophet, to bring forth a new Buddhism suited to the needs of the Chinese or of other peoples in eastern Asia and equipped with the sinews of survival. For all the congresses of Buddhists, official pilgrimages, and so on, I see no signs of a genuine revival. The steady secularization of life throughout eastern Asia makes one suspect that the time of great religious movements may have passed forever. Perhaps the most that can be hoped is that the gentle compassion and respect for others that came from Buddhism will linger as a kind of ethical substratum underlying the secular philosophies, the national cults, the state socialisms of the future.

Another conclusion — one closely linked to the first — is that great religions that may once have served the spiritual needs of millions of people may, like other notable products of the human spirit and intellect, pass away, die out and become the concern only of the historian of religion. Such has been the fate of Manicheanism, Mazdeanism, and other great faiths. Buddhism, for reasons comparable to those we have seen in the Chinese case, will probably fail to adjust to the needs of modern Asian man. Despite scattered evidence to a contrary trend, I would expect Buddhism to pass from life into history.

Last, we might observe that throughout the whole of eastern Asia, the struggle today is for the new nations' survival as economically and politically viable units. The eyes of Asian people are turned to the ideologues who offer to relate present action to future benefits, to the five-year planners, the technicians who seek to bring these people up to the level of life achieved over a period of two hundred crowded years by the West. We should be prepared therefore for a long period of secular faiths, of leadership that talks of economic and political salvation rather than the salvation of souls, of earthly utopias rather than heavenly cities. And all the formulas that compete for men's support will idolize the nation-state to the utter destruction of the principles of cosmopolitan tolerance and compassion which were the great glory of Buddhism in its day.

} JOSEPH M. KITAGAWA {

New Religions in Japan · A Historical Perspective

THE complexity of the contemporary situation in Japan is such that casual observers have extreme difficulty in making any sense out of it. This is especially true with respect to the religious scene in postwar Japan. Some writers, for example, stress the spiritual vitality of the so-called "new religions" (*shinkō shūkyō*) and give the impression that older religions are doomed to fade away. Others are persuaded that the residual strength of Shinto and Buddhism will eventually overcome what they consider to be the temporary popularity of the new religions. Still others suggest that modernization will inevitably drive Japan toward the path of secularization and that no religious tradition, new or old, will long remain as a significant factor in the life of the Japanese people. Undoubtedly there is some truth in each of these views. It is not my concern, however, to deal with these questions directly. Rather I would like to place the contemporary Japanese religious scene in a broader historical perspective by examining how the underlying structure of the Japanese religious heritage — its world of meaning and its mode of apprehending human reality — has undergone changes in the contemporary experience of the Japanese.

27

Historically the development of Japanese religions has been characterized by two seemingly contradictory trends. Seen from one perspective, this history appears to be an unbroken, continuous development from the prehistoric period to the present century. To be sure there have been a number of social, political, and cultural changes which have exerted profound influences on Japanese religions. But the core of the ancient heritage has been preserved more or less intact, so that the Japanese have never experienced any abrupt sense of rupture with the past. Seen from another perspective, however, the history of Japanese religions cannot be understood without taking into account the penetration of a series of religious and philosophical influences from abroad. In a real sense we might see these contradictory trends as the two main threads which have been intricately interwoven into the colorful tapestry of Japanese religious history through the ages. For, consciously or unconsciously, the Japanese have appropriated and indigenized many features of alien religions and thus enriched their own world of meaning, much as they have adopted foreign words and ideas without altering the basic grammatical structure of their language. First, therefore, it is important to make a serious attempt to understand the religious outlook of the early Japanese people and then to examine the historical development of the various religious traditions in Japan.

Early Shinto. Although the term Shinto (the "way of the *kami*, or gods") was coined in the sixth century A.D., I resort to the designation "early Shinto" (for lack of a better term) to refer to the loosely organized religious tradition of prehistoric and early historic Japan. Most scholars agree that the earliest phase of Japanese prehistory, with its sub-Neolithic level of culture, can be traced to the fourth millennium B.C. Then, somewhere around the third century B.C., the arts of rice cultivation, spinning, and weaving, as well as the use of iron, were introduced to Japan. Only in the third or fourth century A.D. did Japan begin to enter the historic period. Evidently throughout the long prehistoric period a number of ethnic groups, mainly from northeast Asia, the Korean peninsula, and various parts of China, infiltrated into the Japanese islands, and this migration of people continued until well into the early phase of the historic period. It is significant to note that toward the latter part of the prehistoric period the inhabitants of the islands seemed to have attained a degree of self-consciousness as one people, sharing a common language and culture.

Unfortunately very little is known about the religious beliefs and practices in the prehistoric period of Japan.[1] For example, the religious influence of the Ainu on the non-Ainu groups cannot be clearly ascertained. Nevertheless there is good reason to portray early Shinto as a simple "cosmic" religion because it accepted the whole of life and the cosmos as sacred, permeated by the *kami* (sacred or divine nature). And like cosmic religions in other parts of the world, early Shinto was nonrational, nonmetaphysical, and ethnocentric, lacking the concept of a universal principle. On the other hand early Shinto was strongly inclined toward aesthetic values, as evidenced by its preoccupation with the beauty and rhythm of nature. While early Shinto did not speculate on the meaning of the mysterious universe, it nevertheless accepted simple mythological accounts about the origin and nature of *kami* (deities), man, and the world (which was equated with the islands of Japan). Early Japanese believed in the existence of a three-dimensional universe, namely, the celestial abode of heavenly *kami*, the earthly domain of human and other beings, and the nether world where unclean spirits were said to reside. It was Amaterasu Ō-mikami, usually referred to as the Sun Goddess and the central deity in the Shinto pantheon, who was believed to have sent her grandson, the mythical ancestor of the imperial clan, to rule Japan.

One of the chief sources for our understanding of early Shinto is its ritual, which has been faithfully handed down from generation to generation. Because Shinto has been reluctant to articulate its doctrinal systems, it has always expressed its beliefs through a series of rituals. In fact all the key concepts of Shinto — for example, *harai* (purification for the removal of defilements, pollutions, and disasters), *musubi* (the creative spirit of birth and becoming), and *tsutsushimi* (a circumspect attitude) — were acted out liturgically long before they were explicated theoretically.

Another important aspect of early Shinto was the system of ancient Japanese social solidarity based on the clan (*uji*). Each clan had its clansmen, men related by ties of kinship; there were also groups of professional persons who were not necessarily related by blood to the clan; and finally there were slaves — all of whom were ruled by the clan chieftain. Each clan was also a unit of religious solidarity centering around the *kami* of the clan (*uji-gami*). (The early Japanese acknowledged the existence of numerous other kinds of *kami* and believed that there were diviners, shamans, healers, and sorcerers who had special skills in dealing with them.) The so-called Yamato kingdom (the old designation of Japan), which established itself around the fourth century A.D., was in effect a confederation of a number of autonomous clans, united by the religious and political power of the imperial clan, which based its claim to authority on solar ancestry. While in the course of history the imperial clan often lost political power, its religious authority was rarely questioned. In this sense early Shinto provided a basic framework for the political structure of Japan, even though its ideal of the "unity of religion and government" (*saisei-itchi*) was not actualized in subsequent periods.

Admittedly our knowledge of the life of the people in the early historic period is limited. We are fortunate, however, to have an eighth-century anthology of poems, the *Manyō-shū* ("Collection of a Myriad Leaves"), because some of its poems give us a glimpse of the beliefs and attitudes of the early Japanese people. Their life was not easy, and they were at the mercy of the capricious power of nature. Yet they found a meager joy in the life of the hamlet and rejoiced in the swift changes of the four seasons. Every aspect of their life was associated with the activities of *kami*, and it is said that "no tree could be marked for felling, no bush tapped for lacquer juice, no oven built for smelting or for pottery, and no forge fire lit without appeal to the *Kami* residing in each." Equally interesting is a description in a Chinese chronicle of the third century A.D., *Wei Chih* ("History of the Kingdom of Wei"). This account states that the Japanese practiced divination by burning bones and that they appointed a diviner who was not allowed to comb his hair, to wash, to eat meat, or to approach women. When a death occurred, the whole family went into the water and washed after the funeral. The Chinese chronicle also mentions a female shaman-ruler in one of the principalities of Japan, an unmarried old woman who devoted herself to magic and sorcery while her brother assisted her in ruling the country.

Apparently the early Japanese did not speculate about the existence of a universal principle behind the celestial, natural, and human phenomena. All human activities were explained and sanctioned in terms of what the *kami*, the ancestors or heroes, did in primordial time. In addition the people lived close to the *kami*, who threatened or blessed them in all their activities. The ruler, even after the consolidation of the Yamato kingdom, did not follow any rational law or system of administration. Instead the sovereign governed according to the unpredictable will of the *kami* as revealed to him through divination and oracles. Indeed what was later designated as Shinto was just this ensemble, which constituted the peculiarly Japanese approach to all aspects of life and the world, an approach which had been shaped and conditioned by the historic experience of the early Japanese people.

Confucianism and Buddhism. The historic situation in the fifth and sixth centuries brought Japan into close contact first with the kingdoms in the Korean peninsula, which were cultural satellites of China, and eventually with China itself, thereby introducing many aspects of Chinese civilization to Japan. The magnitude of the Chinese impact on Japan may be illustrated by the wholesale adoption of Chinese script, historiography, art, architecture, astrology, and astronomy, as well as the philosophical concepts of Taoism and the Yin-yang system. But by far the most important legacies of the Chinese influence were Confucianism and Buddhism.

It should be noted that by the time Confucianism reached Japan it was no longer the simple humanistic philosophy and ethics of Confucius and Mencius. It had developed into a comprehensive approach to life and society, including legal and educational institutions, ethics, and political theory — all based on the universal principle of Tao (*Michi* in Japanese). Understandably Japanese society, which hitherto had been based on primitive communal rules and paternalistic authorities relying primarily on the sanction of *kami*, was compelled to undergo a series of changes under the impact of Confucianism, which had a coherent image of society. Also by the time Buddhism was introduced to Japan this originally humble Indian religion of mendicants and laity had become the bearer of a great civilization, armed with voluminous scriptures, sophisticated philosophical systems, and gigantic ecclesiastical institutions, all based on dharma (*Ho* in Japanese), the universal law of Buddha.

The introduction of two different kinds of universal principles, Tao and dharma, embodied by Confucianism and Buddhism respectively, greatly enriched as well as complicated the religious and cultural development in Japan. But the pious hope of the prince-regent Shōtoku (573–621) to reorganize the government according to Confucian models while promoting Buddhism — without, however, neglecting Shinto — was never fully realized during his time or in subsequent periods. Shortly after Shōtoku's death the government structure was centralized along the lines of the Chinese imperial model, and the affairs of the nation were administered by bureaucrats trained in Confucian learning. Yet the universal Confucian principle of Tao was not accepted as the new foundation of the nation. In fact the legitimacy of this seemingly Sinified government structure was believed to be ultimately sanctioned by the will of the *kami* of the Shinto tradition. Moreover the sovereign came to be regarded as the "manifest *kami*" (*akitsukami*), who governed the nation by a series of imperial rescripts (*Ritsuryō*) which, to be sure, were prepared by the Sinified bureaucrats. The political structure thus developed in the seventh century A.D. on the basis of Shinto-Confucian principles is referred to as the *Ritsuryō* (imperial rescript) state.

Partly as a reaction to what was then considered the excessive Confucian emphasis of the seventh century, especially in governmental and educational activities, eighth-century Japan (the

Nara period) depended heavily on Buddhist inspiration. The imperial court initiated the construction of state-supported Buddhist temples both in the provinces and in the capital city of Nara. A number of prominent Buddhist clerics served as court chaplains or imperial advisers, and one priest even served as the prime minister. In the course of time some of the Buddhist and Shinto deities were homologized, a development that prepared the ground for the de facto amalgamation of Buddhism and Shinto which appeared later on. In the eighth century too a large number of ascetics, shamans, healers, and diviners of the folk Shinto tradition in the countryside came under the nominal influence of Buddhism. These men, untutored in the doctrines and practices of Buddhism, developed as it were their own path of salvation, which was called the path of the holy man (*hijiri*) or the way of the unlicensed Buddhist priest (*ubasoku*).[2] This tradition of shamanistic folk Buddhism was to play an important role in subsequent religious developments in Japan.

With the establishment of a new capital in Kyoto toward the end of the eighth century, the imperial court attempted to reinforce the principles of the seventh-century *Ritsuryō* state. Government control, however, was quickly taken over by the powerful Fujiwara family and later by the retired monarchs, so that the reigning sovereigns were left with only religious authority. It was during the following Heian period (between the ninth and twelfth centuries) that Japan enjoyed the flowering of elegant art and culture so vividly portrayed in the famous *Tale of Genji*. The religious creativity of this period came primarily from Esoteric (Tantric) Buddhism, advocated by the Tendai and the Shingon schools which were introduced from China in the ninth century. Shinto played only a subordinate role in the Buddhist-dominated Ryōbu-Shinto (Shinto-Buddhist amalgamation), and the so-called Mountain Ascetics, who were the heirs of the shamanistic Buddhists of the earlier period, came to ally themselves with Esoteric Buddhism. Ironically, while the Buddhist monastic centers enjoyed wealth, power, and prestige, people in the lower strata of Japanese society received very little spiritual benefit from them.

The picture changed radically in the thirteenth century. The new era was ushered in by the initiative of the feudal lords, who reflected the indigenous pre-*Ritsuryō* spirit of culture and society. The emergence of the new social order under the leadership of the Minamoto warriors also injected rigor and creativity into Japanese Buddhism. It so happened that the age coincided with *mappō*, or the "period of the latter end of law" according to the Buddhist cosmic history. In this situation the leaders of new Buddhist movements, notably those of the Pure Land and the Nichiren schools, advocated the experience of the certainty of salvation, rejecting the traditional monastic rules and ritualism. Side by side with the development of indigenous schools of Buddhism, the Rinzai and Sōtō Zen schools were introduced from China, and their direct, simple teachings and strict mental disciplines quickly won the hearts of the warriors. A nostalgia for ancient Japan was also evident during the short-lived imperial rule (1333–36), but the unrealistic measures taken by the royalists resulted in the formation of a second feudal regime under the Ashikaga warrior clan, which lasted until the sixteenth century. During the turbulent era of the Ashikaga rule it was Zen monks who more than anyone else contributed to art, literature, and education and who inspired the development of the tea cult and the Nō play.

Neo-Confucianism and State Shinto. Neo-Confucianism is a complex semireligious philosophy, blending Confucian and Ch'an (Zen) traditions, which appeared in China during the Sung period. It was transmitted to, and promoted in, Japan by Zen monks, who were then the intellectual elite. When the Tokugawa feudal regime was established at the turn of the seventeenth century, its rulers turned to Neo-Confucianism as a guiding principle for the nation. In a real sense the character of the regime was set by the policy of the first *shōgun* (generalissimo), the feudal ruler Tokugawa Iyeyasu, who was venerated as the earthly manifestation of the "Sun God of the East." [8] And much as the seventh-century *Ritsuryō* state was governed by a series of imperial rescripts carried out by Confucian-trained bureaucrats, so the first Tokugawa *shōgun* issued directives (*hatto*) which were executed by Confucian scholars who were in the service of the regime. The Tokugawas banned Catholicism, which had gained considerable influence during the late sixteenth and early seventeenth centuries in western Japan, and adopted the policy of "national seclusion." The rulers furthermore required every household to belong to a particular Buddhist temple. The Buddhist parochial system, hitherto unknown in Japan, was thus fostered as an arm of the feudal regime for the purpose of thought control.

Meanwhile Confucian scholars, who were for the most part emotionally anti-Buddhist, began to ally themselves with Shinto, which was neglected by the feudal regime. Many Confucianists even equated the *li* (reason or principle) taught by Neo-Confucianism with the "way of the *kami*" of Shinto. The cause of Shinto was also greatly enhanced by the policy of "National Learning," which promoted scholarly investigation of ancient Japanese classics. Shinto was thus reinvigorated during the latter eighteenth and early nineteenth centuries, at a time when the prestige of the Tokugawa regime was steadily declining, in part because of its inability to meet the threat of Western encroachment on Japan. Following the show of force by an American naval squadron led by Commodore Matthew Perry in 1853, the anti-Tokugawa party, including the coalition of Confucian and Shinto elements, toppled the feudal regime and brought about the return of imperial rule under Emperor Meiji, who reigned from 1867 to 1912.

The policy-makers of the Meiji regime, who determined the course of modern Japan, envisaged the establishment of a rich and strong nation-state. To this end they eagerly welcomed various features of Western civilization. It is worth noting, however, that the acceptance of Western knowledge was based on the conviction of Japanese Confucianists that *li* or reason is universal. Moreover, notwithstanding the adoption of a Western-style constitution, parliamentary government, and educational system, the model for modern Japan was sought in the seventh-century *Ritsuryō* state, a highly centralized government reigned over by the divine prerogatives of the sovereign and managed by a corps of bureaucrats trained in the Western arts of political administration.

Much of the contradictory character of modern Japan can be understood in this light. At any rate the Meiji regime ordered the dissolution of the age-old Shinto-Buddhist amalgamation, gave tacit support to the popular anti-Buddhist movement, and lifted the ban against Christianity.

While the principle of freedom of religion within limits was acknowledged in the constitution, the real intent of the government was to superimpose the emperor cult and Shinto over all religions. Thus Shinto, now called State or National Shinto, was controlled directly by the government, while the messianic and healing cults of Shinto tradition were designated as Sect (*kyōha*) Shinto. In addition the government depended heavily on Confucian ethics to provide norms for national, public, and private morality, as evidenced by the imperial rescript on education (promulgated in 1890) and the moral teaching (*shūshin*) that was required in every primary and secondary school. Nevertheless at that time the influence of Western philosophy and political ideology, as well as of Christianity, on the young and educated segments of Japanese society was not negligible. In this situation many Shintoists, Confucianists, and superpatriotic Buddhists joined forces to resist the "threat" of foreign influences. They also rendered enthusiastic support to the expansionist policies of the government during the Sino-Japanese War (1894–1905), the Russo-Japanese War (1904–1905), and the annexation of Korea (1910). By that time the Conference of Three Religions, with Shinto, Buddhist, and Christian representatives, had also been inaugurated to cooperate with the aims of the government.

After the short period of the so-called Taishō Democracy — an era of relative domestic peace, democratic atmosphere, and parliamentary rule, culminating in the passage of the Universal Manhood Suffrage Law in 1925 — Japan faced a series of internal and external crises. A small but active and articulate group of Communist intellectuals campaigned for and supported an ever-growing number of labor strikes. Conversely the League for the Prevention of Communism, the National Foundation Society, and other right-wing groups zealously fought against all "dangerous, foreign ideologies." Soon a menacing alliance between the political parties and militarists began to intimidate the liberals, an alliance which started a chain of military aggression in China and eventually involved Japan in World War II. In this atmosphere a religious league composed of Christian, Buddhist, and Sect Shinto denominations was organized to provide a spiritual bulwark for the nation. All religious groups in Japan were forced to recognize the principle that the authoritarian government, sanctioned by State Shinto, could alone dictate the thought and behavior of every Japanese subject.

New Religions. Japan's defeat in 1945 was undoubtedly the most traumatic event in the historic memory of the Japanese people. Many Japanese questioned then whether their country would ever again become a world power, in spite of its industrial potential, its huge reservoir of skilled workers, and its technological sophistication. Not only did the Japanese experience a temporary loss of nerve as the result of military defeat, but they also felt a great anxiety about the future. They had no idea what to expect from the Allied military occupation symbolized in the person of General of the Army Douglas MacArthur, for it was a new experience for them to live under foreign rule. On his part General MacArthur, nicknamed the "Star-spangled Mikado," issued a series of directives, much as the ancient Japanese monarchs or the Tokugawa *shōgun* had done, ordering the captive Japanese government to enact a constitutional revision, undertake educational and land reforms, release political prisoners, purge political criminals, dismantle the armed forces and the *zaibatsu* (financial oligarchy), and initiate various other measures. Although some of the reforms were ill-conceived and mishandled, the Allied military occupation played a decisive role in transforming Japan in the postwar era. Whether the occupation authorities realized it or not, the course of Japan was determined to a great extent by their policies, and Japan began to orient itself politically, economically, and culturally toward the Western nations, particularly toward the United States.

Among all the changes brought about by the occupation forces, the most radical and far-reaching steps were those relating to the religious foundation of the Japanese nation.[4] That is to say, each one of the enforced measures destroyed religio-political principles which had been taken for granted as sacred and immutable through much of the historic period in Japan. In the first place, the principle of religious liberty undercut the notion, based on the historic Shinto-Confucian synthesis, that every Japanese must pledge his ultimate loyalty to the throne and the nation. What was involved was more than the freedom to worship and to form religious associations; the principle of religious liberty also affirmed the individual's freedom, if need be, to obey higher principles than the laws of the government. Second, the directive that disestablished State Shinto prohibited the "sponsorship, support, perpetuation, control, and dissemination of Shinto by the Japanese national, prefectural, and local government, or by public officials." This meant the repudiation of the special prerogatives of Shinto accorded by the government from time immemorial, first articulated by the seventh-century *Ritsuryō* state and then reinforced by the Meiji regime, which in effect had created a new superreligion of State Shinto.

Finally, the principle of separation of religion and state disavowed what had been regarded as sacred principle from the time of early Shinto, namely, the notion of the unity of religion and government (*saisei-itchi*). On the basis of this principle Prince Shōtoku in the seventh century had forged a multireligious policy, assigning different roles to Shinto, Confucianism, and Buddhism, and monarchs in the eighth century had espoused Buddhism as the religion of the state. Similarly the Tokugawa regime banned Catholicism on the ground that it was irreconcilable with the policy of the regime. Even the Meiji regime, which gave lip service to the cause of religious freedom within limits, did not hesitate to declare that the heavenly *kami* and the sun goddess had established the throne and made the succession secure. As one commentator has noted, "the line of emperors in unbroken succession entered into possession thereof and handed it on. Religious ceremonies and government" were one and the same (*saisei-itchi*) ."[5] It was on

38

this basis that State Shinto had been concocted as a superreligion, overarching all other religions. Given such a historical background, one can readily understand the profound effect the principle of separation of religion and state had on the transformation of Japan.

Equally significant was the imperial rescript issued in 1946, which stated: "The ties between us and our people have always stood upon mutual trust and affection. They do not depend upon mere legends and myths. They are not predicated on the false conception that the Emperor is divine and that the Japanese people are superior to other races and fated to rule the world." [6] The wording of this rescript was couched in traditional phrases, but its contents clearly indicated that the traditional world of meaning of the Japanese, their understanding of history which derived ultimately from the sacred sanctions of the ancient Shinto myths, could no longer be preserved in postwar Japan. Thus the Japanese people were cut off abruptly from their own past, especially from the underlying spiritual orientation of the world view which they had inherited from the ancient cosmic religious outlook. I do not suggest that this radical rupture with the past was necessarily undesirable; I do believe, however, that it helps to explain why many Japanese, haunted by uncertainties about their own identity, are looking for viable options which might provide them with some kind of certainty, hope, and faith.

The significance of the new religions which have mushroomed since the end of World War II lies in the fact that no matter how unsophisticated they may be, they claim to offer a coherent meaning for life and the world to people who feel lost because they sense an abrupt rupture with the old and familiar world of yesterday. In this connection it should be remembered that throughout the historic period, side by side with the established religious tradition supported by the state and adhered to by the elite, there were other types of religious orientation espoused by the people. Some of them, from the shamanistic folk Buddhist groups of the eighth century to the messianic cults of the twentieth century, were persecuted, while others, like the new Buddhist movements in the thirteenth century, were barely tolerated by the authorities.

These spontaneous religious cults and movements for the most part lacked the benefits of sophisticated doctrinal systematization and varied in their outlook and orientation. However, they offered their adherents not only a sense of belonging and certain this-worldly or other-worldly benefits, but also simple and direct access to the sacred ground of life. And the fact that a large number of quasi religions (*ruiji shūkyō*) continued to emerge in the nineteenth and twentieth centuries despite rigid governmental restrictions clearly demonstrates the tenacity of the spontaneous religious tradition on the folk and mass levels in Japan. Some of them were dissolved by the order of the government, while others were forced to go underground. Only those which affiliated themselves with some of the Sect Shinto denominations managed to survive before and during the war. And, although it was far from the intent of the occupation authorities, the principle of religious liberty which they initiated released the hitherto submerged religious energy of the folk and mass levels in the form of the new religions.

There were to be sure other factors — sociological, psychological, economic — involved in the sudden eruption of many new religious groups. Certainly the loss of potential leaders in the older religious traditions during the war, the land reform which seriously affected many of the Buddhist temples and Shinto shrines, and the mobility of the population which undermined the Shinto and Buddhist parochial systems, to cite only the obvious, made it easier for the new religious groups to emerge and to carry on their activities. Then too both Protestant and Catholic Christianity, which appeared to be popular during the early days of the occupation, did not succeed in gaining a grass-roots base, partly because of a general resentment against its foreignness and partly because of the tacit support, real or imagined, it received from the officials of the occupation. Be that as it may, from our point of view it is impossible to understand the significance of the phenomenon of the new religions unless we take seriously the religious factors involved.

It may be a truism to point out that the so-called new religions are not really new in terms of their religious ethos and orientation, although they make full use of modern techniques of organization, administration, and propaganda. For the most part they betray the shamanistic and messianic features inherited from the folk and mass religious movements: a strong thrust of this-worldly eschatology and soteriology, heavy dependence on such magico-religious practices as healing and divination, and the use of familiar moral axioms concerned with honesty, filial piety, and industriousness.[7] Their doctrines are simple and eclectic, presented in a language which is readily understandable even by the uneducated.

The most conspicuous feature of these groups is the charismatic quality of the founders or systematizers, who embody many of the characteristics of a savior figure. Their utterances are accepted as revelations from the *kami*, and their biographies are embroidered by pious imagination. Moreover their birthplaces or places of residence are believed to be the "center of the world," formerly hidden from human eyes but now revealed. In sharp contrast to their indifference to doctrinal sophistication, they have devised rituals for every need and occasion, from small intimate gatherings of the faithful for mutual exhortation to mass meetings conducted with much fanfare. As far as the adherents are concerned, they receive in faith the assurance that through the charismatic leaders and their holy communities the saving power of the *kami* touches, guides, and sanctifies all aspects of life.

In the main the outlook of the new religions toward the present and the future of Japan may be characterized as one of naïve optimism. Even though many of their spokesmen pontificate at the drop of a hat on domestic and international problems, touching on every conceivable subject from population control and nuclear testing to unemployment, education, and East-West tensions, their assessment of issues is simplistic and unrealistic, and they tend to solve today's complex problems with yesterday's pious solutions. They do, however, approach all dimensions of life holistically instead of dividing it into a series of separate compartments. This may account for their unwillingness to divorce religion from politics, although only the Sōka Gakkai, which now prefers to be equated with the Nichiren-Shō school of Buddhism, has thus far attained conspicuous success on the political scene.

Considering the number of the new religions, their relationships with one another have been on the whole rather peaceful, even though serious rivalries do exist. While some derived their original inspiration from Buddhist sources, their cooperation with Buddhist schools has been practically nonexistent, with the possible exception of the Nichiren-related religions. Nevertheless their influence on Shinto and various schools of Buddhism has not been negligible, since the older faiths cannot successfully ignore the rising new groups. They can no longer remain idle, but must actively consolidate their folds in order to deter the further encroachment of the new religions. Conversely, some of the new religions, which are now showing signs of institutionalization, have begun to sense the danger of counter-influence from the older traditions. In short, while the older religions are compelled to try to keep up with the new religions, some of the new religions are losing the freshness and vitality they possessed two decades ago.

In all fairness we must appreciate the built-in tendencies toward ethnocentricism on the part of the new religions. Unlike Buddhism and Christianity, which are self-consciously aware of their participation in the global communities of their respective faiths, the new religions, not unlike Shinto in this respect, have no recourse but to view everything from their own perspective. Apparently the fact that the ethos of the new religions was nurtured by the long experience of the folk and mass religious tradition enabled them to reach a large number of people quickly and easily in the aftermath of World War II, when many Japanese were tormented by uncertainties and anxieties. But with the passage of time people have begun to recover from their temporary loss of nerve, while at the same time they have become keenly aware of the staggering problems — cultural, social, economic, and political — which confront Japan today and will continue to do so for years to come. Many Japanese are persuaded that the fundamental problem of Japan is not, as some Western analysts seem to feel, the simple cultural schizophrenia of a people caught between the East and the West.

New Religions in Japan

Rather the real issue for Japan is how to develop its own style and method of modernization, without resorting in toto to either the capitalist or the Communist formula. It remains to be seen whether the new religions — or other religions for that matter — can assist in this task, or whether they will unwittingly or otherwise serve primarily as spiritual tranquilizers, in effect contributing to social, political, cultural, and, more fundamentally, religious inertia.

REFERENCES

1. For a more detailed discussion of this subject, see my "Prehistoric Background of Japanese Religion," *History of Religions*, 2 (Winter 1963): 292-328.

2. On *hijiri* and *ubasoku*, see Ichiro Hori, "On the Concept of Hijiri (Holy Man)," *Numen*, 5 (April, September 1958): 128-60, 199-232.

3. Elsewhere I have characterized the Tokugawa regime as a form of "immanental theocracy." See my *Religion in Japanese History* (New York: Columbia University Press, 1966), pp. 154ff.

4. On the religious situation in postwar Japan, see *ibid.*, chap. 6, "Old Dreams or New Vision?"

5. Quoted in Daniel C. Holtom, *Modern Japan and Shinto Nationalism*, 2nd ed. (Chicago: University of Chicago Press, 1947), p. 6.

6. The complete text of this rescript is cited in U.S. Department of State, *Occupation of Japan: Policy and Progress*, Publication no. 2671, Far Eastern Series 17 (Washington, D.C., n.d.), pp. 133-35.

7. On the religious characteristics of the new religions, see Ichiro Hori, *Folk Religion in Japan: Community and Change*, ed. Joseph M. Kitagawa and Alan L. Miller (Chicago: University of Chicago Press, 1968), chap. 6, "The New Religions and the Survival of Shamanic Tendencies."

) I. MILTON SACKS (

Some Religious Components in Vietnamese Politics

ALMOST every discussion of Vietnam in recent years has consisted largely of a manipulation of symbols, based on whether the speakers were for or against the American commitment in Southeast Asia. There has been, generally speaking, little discussion about the society and one has the sense, curiously enough, that the more we have talked about *Vietnam*, the less we know about the *Vietnamese*. The aim of this essay therefore is to focus on a historical description of Vietnam and its religious groupings in a way that may provide some partial explanation of what has actually been occurring in Vietnam during the recent past. The area to be considered is essentially that of South Vietnam, although some general remarks will be made about North Vietnam as well.

In any attempt to understand events in Vietnam, it is important to keep in mind that the country's years of contact with China, dating back to the first millennia of Vietnamese existence, saw the importation of the Confucian state pattern, together with its entire system of values. The governmental system in Vietnam came to be characterized by the same convergence of political, legislative, and religious power, vested in a sovereign emperor who was assisted by a mandarin bureaucracy, as that which prevailed in China. The principal units of the social structure were the family system, the semiautonomous village, and the central state authority. In addition the Vietnamese state, like that of China, was conceptualized in magical and religious terms, as "the symbol of a world order, and the expression of a system of proprieties in human and superhuman relationships." * In such a society the intimate relations between the forces of nature and the well-being of an agricultural society found expression in unified and integrated political and religious concepts. Religious practices mirrored the necessity for a harmonious relationship between man and his environment as well as among men, lest calamity befall all. At the apex of the system, the emperor combined both political and religious functions. In such a system either religious or political dissidence involved potential disruption of the total system.

This interpenetration of religious belief and social ethics and behavior was one reason for the sporadic governmental persecution of Buddhism, Taoism, and, later, Christianity. The mandarinate viewed all heterodoxy as a challenge to its power. As a result of governmental persecution of unorthodox beliefs, Buddhist and Taoist teachers often became the chief organizers of secret societies. This reaction was inevitable since only through the formation of secret societies could dissenting movements be developed. Because the secret societies grew in response to a situation created by an authoritarian society in which religion and politics were indissoluble, their development reflected that situation. They too tended to be hierarchical in their basic structure, and their rituals were pervaded by prevailing religious customs. A Vietnamese who joined them was an individual whose every act fitted into a cosmogeny, whether a well-defined one or an eclectic mixture of several religious practices. The aim of Taoist and Buddhist dissidents was always to replace the existing dynasty with a new one and to effect a change in the religious, political, and social structure in

* Cora DuBois, *Social Forces in Southeast Asia.* Minneapolis: University of Minnesota Press, 1949. P. 31.

Vietnam. Thus the Vietnamese have been peculiarly vulnerable to the appeals of total ideological systems. It is this search for a new key to the universe which helps in large measure to explain the rapid spread of Marxism, socialism, and fascism among Vietnamese intellectuals.

Like Buddhism and Taoism, Christianity too was viewed with disfavor by the mandarinate. Since it was brought to Vietnam by representatives of European powers whose drive for commercial and political advantage in Asia could scarcely be camouflaged, whatever the purity of their religious motivations, it is easy to understand the negative reaction of the Vietnamese court. In addition, the recognition that Christianity incorporated beliefs that struck at the moral foundations of a Confucian society led the mandarinate to condemn it as a purely subversive doctrine. From the time of its appearance in Vietnam early in the sixteenth century, Catholicism and its native adherents were regarded suspiciously as a possible channel for antinational activity.

This reaction to Catholicism has extended to the modern period, and there still remains an uneasy relationship between the Catholic hierarchy, whether foreign or native born, and the Vietnamese nationalists of Buddhist and other persuasions. Catholicism is felt to represent an alien force in ways that even the new versions of Buddhism, to be discussed below, do not exhibit in Vietnamese society. Nevertheless the acceptance of Christianity by some Vietnamese led to the creation of a significant Catholic minority in the development of organic communities in Vietnam. The priest became in effect the leader of his flock of believers at the village level. The Catholics, as we shall see, have become an important religious group in modern nationalist politics.

Religion and politics have thus been intertwined since the earliest period of Vietnamese existence. A consciousness of nationhood first emerged as a consequence of the early struggle by the Vietnamese to establish a society that was independent of Chinese political rule even while it was based on the model provided by Chinese Confucianism. The success of the traditional society in maintaining an independent existence was predicated on the ability of the monarchy and the mandarinate to mobilize support from the peasantry. Peasant communities traditionally enjoyed considerable autonomy with respect to the state, and the primary link of the ruling group to its peasant base was established through the medium of Confucian ideology — a cosmogony that brought order out of the chaos of men's relationships to each other, to society, and to nature. The shock provided by the inability of Vietnamese society to resist French domination in the nineteenth century promoted both a new awareness of the West and a search for a new basis of national identity.

It was in fact just this search for national identity which so weighed on the political, social, and religious development of the nation which was to become Vietnam. The quest was made complex by two interacting factors. It will be recalled that the Vietnamese, or Annamese as they were designated before the modern period of division and independence, were never inventors. Any religion that was to be a factor in their total societal development necessarily came to them from outside, at least in its purer forms. A second important element in their earlier development — and one which still has its repercussions — was the tendency of the people of the area to clothe the imported religious ideas, and in fact social, political, and even economic ideas, with a Vietnamese character, a tendency resulting frequently in an extremism.

The events which followed on the French takeover of the Indochina area are not only complex but marked by diversity. Extremism in religion, for example, may be seen in the swing toward Catholicism, a religion long in the area, but one that for obvious reasons was given strength and support by the French administration; in the revitalization of older forms, Confucianism and orthodox Buddhism, both Theravada and Mahayana; and also in the development of syncretistic faiths in which old elements were lent new symbols. In a sense the patterns which emerge continue down to the present day. It is difficult, precisely because of the diversity of threads, to treat even the superficialities of the history of the past centuries with precision. Here we can do little more than suggest a relevant chronology.

Thus at the outset of the French colonial occupation, the mandarinate's failure to withstand the impact of European military power and technology laid bare the incompetence of traditional Vietnamese society to cope with the modern world. Although the mandarins' heroic resistance was to contribute to the legends of nationalist struggle, these traditional leaders were unable to mobilize the peasants to stand against the inroads of the modern world, and the mandarinate itself became an anachronistic survival. All that remained of the Vietnamese national heritage was a legacy of characteristic methods of struggle passed on by tradition and employed in the setting of a modern movement. In this situation Vietnamese nationalists felt the need for a new cosmogony to replace the Confucian one historically inherited from the Chinese. The early Vietnamese modernizer and reform leader Pham Quinh attempted to invigorate Confucianism by calling attention to those aspects of it which emphasized humanity and justice, and the accompanying virtues of respect and benevolence. It is of interest to note that this concept was later used by President Ngo Dinh Diem to justify his rule and to promote the stability of his regime in the period from 1955 through 1963. But at no time in the colonial experience did Confucianism itself develop a revolutionary nationalism opposed to the French rule.*

Disappointed with the prospect of gradualist reform under the French during the period after World War I, intellectuals were inclined to turn to modernized versions of traditional Buddhism such as the Cao Dai and the Hoa Hao movements. Each group sought a new vehicle, a new form, and even a new content for their views of nationalism. One early nationalist revolt was an outgrowth of the activities of secret Buddhist societies in Cochin China. (During the seventeenth century the population of this area had become a fusion of the invading Vietnamese and the local residents, who retained many of their earlier religious beliefs.)

* One is almost tempted to say that the only group that has responded to the need to revitalize Confucianism is the Communist leadership in Vietnam, which has in a sense adapted Confucianism to a new form, at least in respect to their conception of leadership and the manner in which they have created hierarchical organization.

Buddhist secret societies in Cochin China opposed the reign of the Nguyen dynasty, regarding it as having capitulated to the French. Pham Sic Long, pretender to the throne of Annam, became the chief leader of these secret societies. After an unsuccessful insurrectionary attempt against the French in 1913, Pham was jailed in the Saigon central prison. Through agents, he was able to build a network of secret organizations throughout Cochin China. There were religious elements in this movement. Pham's supporters believed that he possessed the "Mandate of Heaven" and that he would receive the aid of divine spirits in overcoming the French superiority of force. His followers were given magic potions to make them invulnerable to French arms. The movement culminated in an insurrection early in 1916 which included an attack on the Saigon prison in an attempt to liberate Pham. The French were obliged to suppress the uprising through military action. Pham's revolt against the French used the older frame of Buddhism but also showed the role of the secret society as a movement of dissidence. Such a combination of religion and politics extends into the modern era, for this early involvement of secret Buddhist societies in a political conspiracy was not qualitatively different from the activities of more recent Buddhist sects such as Cao Dai and Hoa Hao, which emerged in Cochin China.

These two sects, along with the Roman Catholics and the Buddhists, constitute the four principal religious groupings which possess effective political organization and support in Vietnam today. Excluded here as major political-religious movements are the mountain peoples, who have their own particular religion but do not constitute, except in a minor sense, a political force that can be termed religious. Although a large proportion of the Montagnards in South Vietnam were affiliated in a movement called the United Front of Liberation for Mountain Peoples, their organization lacked any common religious bond and was political in an ethnic rather than a religious sense. There is also a Cambodian minority of about 500,000 people in South Vietnam who are Theravada Buddhists, but who are not united in a functioning religious organization and do not play a significant role in Theravada Buddhist organizations. They exist simply as an ethnic group living in a particular area, obtaining special dispensation from the South Vietnamese leadership for representation in the parliamentary system which now exists. What is significant about the Cao Dai, the Hoa Hao, the Roman Catholics, and the Buddhists is that they constitute a large part of the religious life of South Vietnam and have succeeded in organizing influential political groupings there. These four groups, and particularly the first two, require fuller discussion.

The Cao Dai. The Cao Dai movement — the words mean "Supreme Palace" or "High Altar" — began in 1919 when the new faith was revealed in the course of a seance to the Cochin Chinese spiritualist, Ngo Van Chieu. Its elaborate dogma combines elements of the principal religions practiced in Indochina, i.e., Buddhism, Confucianism, Taoism, and Christianity, as well as ancestor and spirit worship. The religion is defined as the third "amnesty" of God, the first amnesty having as its principal figures Moses and Jesus, and the second including Buddha and Lao-tzu. Cao Dai, the third amnesty, is considered to be the highest evolution of the human spirit, because no human being as such represents the religion in a way that is characteristic of the two first amnesties. Instead the voice of the Almighty speaks in the seance through any one of a number of devotees. Cao Dai is a spiritualistic rather than a human-based religion, and to the Vietnamese who profess this faith it has a higher reality and a more spiritual character to it than religions which speak through individuals in the service of the Almighty. Along with Moses, Jesus, Buddha, and Lao-tzu, Cao Dai also respects Victor Hugo and a number of other celebrities, including the French admiral Jean Decoux who administered Vietnam for the Japanese during World War II. There is thus a host of both major and minor spiritual figures in its pantheon, creating a syncretism suggestive of India.

In Cao Dai there have arisen organic communities, meaning in effect that everyone in the community more or less practices the religion and respects the local Cao Dai officials. These peasant communities tend to be impervious to influence from the outside.

There are of course Cao Dai groups in urban areas, but they lack the kind of holistic community that is typical of peasant groups.

The religion was formally organized in 1926 by a Cochin Chinese notable, Le Van Trung, with the assistance of other disciples. Trung was a well-to-do man who devoted his life and his wealth to the organization. Following the example of the Buddha, he renounced a luxurious and licentious existence in favor of a spiritual one. This pattern of conversion and renunciation plays an enormous role in the thinking of peasants, particularly in Vietnam, and relates to a fundamental orientation toward life. The magical elements of spiritualism in the new religion were also attractive to uneducated and credulous peasants.

The organization of Cao Daiism resembles that of the Catholic Church. The chief of the sect is called the pope and presides over the holy seat of the religion at a small village near Tay Ninh City. In 1937 the pope built an impressive cathedral at the foot of a mountain close to Tay Ninh, an edifice which rises high on the mountain and dominates the plain below. In the Buddhist cosmogony such high places are important sites for temples, lending a closeness to the Supreme Being. Cao Dai resurrected a series of important Buddhist behavior patterns for its followers. Its dogma is complex, but it may be sufficient to note that there are sumptuary rules, such as those requiring vegetarianism, as well as rules for social relationships and for behavior toward animals.

It is also of interest that Cao Dai includes female ecclesiastical dignitaries in its hierarchy. Whereas the Confucian pattern of Vietnamese society stresses the patrilineal and the patriarchal, the underlying roots of the social structure (which go back to the Southeast Asian–Malaysian character of the Vietnamese peoples) place more stress on the female role and matrilineal descent. In this sense Cao Dai returns to an earlier pattern, but in another sense, by formally giving sanction and place to women in society, it may be considered a modernizing religion.

Half ancestral and half European, Cao Dai is both syncretistic and modernizing. It attempts to bring the Vietnamese peasant into a new kind of cosmological relationship, making him accept a modernizing influence and at the same time manipulating him by reenforcing the patterns of tradition. Cao Daiism is a religious and social movement and not primarily a political party. Nevertheless its leaders and followers have been active in Vietnamese political life and therefore exercise considerable influence. From its birth Cao Daiism found a favorable ground for its development among the Cochin Chinese intellectuals, particularly the disappointed nationalists. A great many government officials, students, and landowners embraced its teaching.

As might be expected, the movement came under sharp scrutiny by the French authorities, who suspected it of being a cover for subversive nationalist activities. It also encountered strong opposition from the Catholic church, which viewed this rapidly growing rival with considerable alarm. Its spread into Annam and Cambodia was prohibited by the French authorities, but in fact it did reach the southern portions of central Vietnam in subsequent years. In the eyes of many nationalists the initials "C. D." stood not only for Cao Dai but also for "Cuong De." Cuong De was a pretender to the throne of Annam, an exiled nationalist who lived in Japan and who directed from abroad an organization called the Vietnam Restoration Association (later the League). It was believed and said by many, although never stated in any of the official statutes, that the words Cao Dai were simply a means of saying Cuong De. The act of joining the organization thus implied a conceptual affiliation not only with a religious organization but also with a group trying to restore the nation. The linkage is clear; here is a religion which is reviving and rebuilding Buddhism and at the same time is restoring the old empire that was independent of external rule.

From its beginnings as a haven for disappointed reform nationalists, Cao Dai expanded into a movement that counted 100,000 followers by 1932 and some 300,000 by 1934. Thereafter there were internal struggles for control of the organization directed against the pope, Le Van Trung. With his death in 1934, a full-fledged struggle for leadership broke out within the ranks of the hierarchy. Pham Cong Tac, who had built up a secret sect for political and social activity, seized control of the central temple at Tay Ninh and installed himself as interim pope. The Cao Daiists split into a number of distinct sects, the most influential of which was that centered at Tay Ninh. In spite of these divisions the movement continued to grow. Claims of as many as two million adherents have been made, but in view of the number of internal divisions an accurate count is well-nigh impossible.

The various subsects maintained open relations with the legal political movements as well as secret relations with the Japanese from 1934 until 1941. Prominent nationalists were associated with the Tay Ninh sect. Another important sect, the Ben Tre — influential in the provinces of Ben Tre and Tra Vinh — had as its chief Ninh Nga Tung, who was the brother-in-law of the leader of the Constitutionalist Party, a moderate nationalist group that was one of the legal political parties. A third sect, Tien Tien — centered in Gia Dinh, adjacent to Saigon, and influential in neighboring areas — had two prominent pro-Japanese members: Nguyen Van Thai, who attempted to establish relations with the exiled prince Cuong De in Japan in 1940 and was sentenced to five years' imprisonment, and Nguyen Pha Tong, a member of Cuong De's Vietnam Restoration League who fled to Japan and became one of the prince's bodyguards. A fourth sect, the Lien Hoa, had as its principal promoter Nguyen Phan Long, a well-known journalist and leader of the Constitutionalist Party. This was the only Cao Daiist group which had a propaganda organ, a journal entitled *True Religion*. Several other subsects, about twelve in number, were scattered throughout Cochin China. One of them, it might be noted, has had, since the end of World War II, the support of the various Vietnamese Communist movements in the south; this subsect was located on the Ca Mau peninsula, in the very southern part of South Vietnam.

The growth of Cao Dai as a political force and its connections with the Japanese made it a matter of serious concern to the colonial administration. On August 26, 1940, the French authorities in Cochin China instituted formal proceedings to close the temple at Tay Ninh and other Cao Dai installations. A year later Pope

Pham Cong Tac was exiled to Madagascar with a number of his principal associates. These activities by the French did not, however, prevent the Japanese from using the Cao Daiist movement as a cover for their promotion of the Greater East Asia Co-Prosperity Sphere. Throughout World War II the Cao Dai movement played an important role in political events in Indochina.

The Hoa Hao. The development of the Hoa Hao both as a religion and as a political force parallels, at least from the beginning of World War II, the development of Cao Dai, and the same considerations hold true for it. The Hoa Hao religion was founded by the so-called "mad monk," Huynh Phu So. He was born in 1919, the son of a well-to-do peasant who was president of the Catholic notables of his native village, Hoa Hao, in the province of Chaudoc, near the Cambodian border. A sickly young man, Huynh Phu So received religious training for a period of time in an effort to restore his health. In May 1939, at the age of 20, he underwent a violent nervous paroxysm, and, emerging from it, declared that he was cured. Announcing himself as a man who had seen the light, he suddenly began to speak in parables and to preach a new religion. He presented himself as the reincarnation of Nguyen Trung Truc, a Vietnamese hero who was killed during the struggle against the French in 1875. Through this and other claimed incarnations, Huynh Phu So established a link with older sects that had existed in the area for a century or more and provided himself not only with a religious image but also with a well-defined political role. The new teacher stressed as the basis of his religion a primary simplicity of rites and an essentially renovated form of Buddhism. He taught that the Almighty could be invoked by direct contact at any time or place and that neither temples nor a priestly hierarchy were required. The religion is, so to speak, a Buddhist form of Unitarianism.

The doctrines of Hoa Hao are of importance in defining the nature of the sect. There are four major precepts: to honor one's parents; to love one's country; to respect Buddhism and its teachings; to love one's fellow man. ("Buddhism," of course, means respect for the teachings of Huynh Phu So.) There are no temples, but the equivalent of Christian Science reading rooms sprang up over much of South Vietnam, where instruction was given in the teachings of the master. The major precepts, stated in the form of parables, couplets, and verses, incorporated other teachings which could be interpreted as straight nationalist propaganda. Among them were prophecies of the fall of France, the Japanese occupation, and even the coming of the Americans — a remarkable feat considering that Huynh Phu So wrote in 1940. Such predictions enhanced his stature as a religious figure.

Great numbers of South Vietnamese peasants joined the movement and by the end of 1939 several tens of thousands of believers could be counted. These peasant disciples came to regard Huynh Phu So as the reincarnation of the famous figure, Nguyen Van Huyen, a religious dignitary of Tay Yan, who had preached in the reign of Emperor Minh Mang, 1820–41, and who recited poetry, predicted the future, and cured the sick. Such a reputation, based on historical beliefs, furthered the acceptance of the new teacher. In 1940 Huynh Phu So extended his missionary efforts to other provinces in Cochin China, and among his prominent disciples were rich landowners and others who had been cured by the master. So great was his reputation that he was actually called the Fat Song, the "living Buddha," and by the end of the year he had attracted some 100,000 followers in the ten provinces of the delta areas of South Vietnam.

By this time the French authorities began to concern themselves with Huynh Phu So's activities. There had been a marked growth in anti-French underground political activity in South Vietnam at this time, and his teachings contributed to the general unrest. Consequently he was incarcerated in a psychiatric hospital at Cho Quan for treatment for a ten-month period, beginning in August 1940. This imprisonment only served to make a martyr of him, and his reputation rose even higher when he converted the doctor who was treating him. In May 1941 he was transferred to Bac Lieu, a town in the south, where he was kept in residence under police surveillance. His house became a center for pilgrimages of the faithful, who were rewarded by the master with religious addresses interspersed with anti-French pronouncements.

Before long, the French decided it would be desirable to resettle Huynh Phu So in Laos. In the meantime, however, he had also attracted the attention of the Japanese, who had other plans for the successful religious leader.* Several days before the time set by the French for his removal to Laos, a group of his disciples, aided by the Kempetai (the Japanese secret police organization), abducted him and took him to Saigon. There he was housed under the protective custody of the Kempetai, which defended its action by classifying him as a Chungking spy — he was thus represented as a Chinese nationalist being kept under surveillance by the Japanese. The French authorities protested, but the Japanese turned a deaf ear to their remonstrances.

The Japanese political police were anxious to use Huynh Phu So's 100,000-member organization in anti-French intrigues, but as events developed, their activities in behalf of the Vietnamese nationalists were constrained by larger considerations of Japanese diplomatic policy vis-à-vis the French. Nevertheless, the use of Cao Daiists as an auxiliary force by the Japanese army gave them training and discipline. By the end of 1944, as it became clear that the Japanese and the Vichy French in Vietnam were coming to a parting of the ways both the Cao Dai and the Hoa Hao, as well as other nationalists, were clearly making preparations for future bids to power.

Cao Dai and Hoa Hao as Political Forces. The Cao Dai and Hoa Hao movements represented the first successful efforts of non-Communist nationalists in South Vietnam to establish political bases within the masses of the peasantry. In the urbanized areas of Vietnam, of course, there were vigorous radical and reform nationalist movements as well as a very vigorous Communist movement. But in the countryside the sects represented the only politi-

* It will be recalled that with the defeat of France by Nazi Germany, French colonies were connected to the Vichy regime. The result was to allow Japanese military and secret police into Indochina, a prelude to the Japanese takeover of Southeast Asia and Indonesia in 1942. Vichy France retained nominal control of Indochina until 1945.

cal effort. The Catholic Church, it is true, had developed a movement among the peasantry, but its bases were not political. Association with Catholic groups implied the acceptance of a modernizing and Western religion; it was an adaptation to the presence of the French and an attempt to probe the mysteries and the secrets of the conquerors. This meant taking the religion of the conqueror as part of the Vietnamese way of life, but it had no overtly political aspect until later, when the various Catholic groups were swept up by the growing nationalist ideology. Cao Dai and Hoa Hao, on the other hand, were clearly established as half-political, half-religious organizations to provide a means of mobilizing the peasantry.

Individuals involved in the leadership of the sects were urban intellectuals, either revolutionary- or reform-minded, who had been disappointed by their inability to sway the urban population of either the south or the north. In effect they turned to the peasants and the peasant organizations because of their dissatisfaction with nationalist or revolutionary activity in the urban centers. It was not surprising to find in 1967 that the leadership of the Hoa Hao included people who, twenty years earlier, had been members of revolutionary national movements in South Vietnam. They "got" religion after they had lost their earlier religion of radicalism.

Time was to show that these movements had a fatal flaw. Unlike the Communists, the religionists had no concept of an organizing principle for modern Vietnam. They knew how to mobilize the peasants: they could reorganize them in terms of peasant life at the village level, they could introduce the ideas of equality and justice, they could establish hierarchical organizations — all of which were suitable to the older Vietnam. Perhaps their concepts were adequate for creating a more egalitarian and fairer society, but they had no notion of what might serve as a means for modernizing the Vietnamese people, or what might appeal to the people of the urban areas. Later events proved that they could maintain themselves only as isolated, though extensive, groups in the rural areas with no real impact on the urban population. This does not mean, of course, that they could not play a significant political role.

The more recent history of both the Cao Dai and the Hoa Hao can be summarized briefly. Both groups received arms from the Vichy French in the 1944–45 period. Their military formations played an important role in the events of March 1945, when the Japanese suddenly moved to dispossess the French in Vietnam. The sects received support from the first, short-lived government established by Emperor Bao Dai from March through August 1945. Subsequently, when the August revolution took place in the north, they joined other nationalist groups in supporting the new government of Ho Chih Minh in Hanoi. In the south they created a united nationalist front, one that included some additional sects and a host of other political organizations. The subsequent co-operation with the Communists in South Vietnam — where, unlike the situation in the north, the sects and similar nationalist groups were a dominant force and the Communists very weak — led to competition with the left for leadership within the newly established governing committees. For a time there was some hostility between the Cao Dai and the Hoa Hao as they jockeyed with the Communist leadership, but generally speaking they worked with the Viet Minh against the French.

In the period after June 1946, because of the Communist desire to incorporate their following into a unified grouping under their own control, the Cao Dai and the Hoa Hao broke with them. Forced to choose between the French on the one hand and the Communists on the other, both the Cao Dai and the Hoa Hao worked out a truce with the French. This truce permitted them to receive military and financial aid from the French and also gave them virtual autonomy in large areas of the western portion of South Vietnam. Each group thus came to have a territorial base in the areas which it controlled; in fact, their territorial bases were so firm and they were so little bothered by either the French or the Viet Minh (who found it wiser to concentrate against the French than to fight other nationalist groupings) that they began to compete with each other. As they extended their organizing efforts into the peasant villages, Cao Dai and Hoa Hao groups engaged in a number of bloody clashes. Eventually a pact was signed which defined the territorial limits of each group into what could be called two kingdoms in South Vietnam.

As the military position of the French weakened, and as they relinquished authority in favor of the imperial role of Emperor Bao Dai, the Cao Daiists turned to the French for more material aid and more arms. They requested, for example, support for a 45,000-man army, receiving in fact enough money and weapons to create a force of 15,000 to 20,000 men. They became the official tax collectors for the government in the areas which they controlled and in 1949 were given several high cabinet posts in the Bao Dai government. The Hoa Hao moved along much the same lines. At the same time that the Cao Dai and Hoa Hao enlarged their holdings, they adopted a policy of not fighting the Viet Minh, on the principle that there was no point in wasting precious military forces in a futile struggle against the Viet Minh when the Viet Minh itself was busy fighting the French. Their idea appears to have been to let those two opponents destroy each other, with the hope of reaping the harvest thereafter. This kind of calculation was not very different from that which prevailed in parts of China, where the Communists permitted the nationalists and the Japanese to fight each other while they themselves picked up territory that eluded control of the two major antagonists. In Vietnamese history one often finds that when numerous sects contend with each other, the way is paved for the leadership of others.

In 1953 when French support of the sects began to wane, the Cao Dai and the Hoa Hao suddenly offered to conciliate the struggle between Bao Dai and Ho Chih Minh. On the basis of tentative arrangements dating as early as 1948, the leadership of the two sects had generally agreed not only that they would not fight each other but that they would cooperate in the development of a so-called United Front of Action. They further agreed to coordinate political efforts vis-à-vis the French and the Communists. But in 1953, recognizing that Bao Dai was weak, and that the Communists might be in process of winning a victory over the French and might in fact emerge as the dominant force, the Cao Dai and Hoa Hao leadership proposed itself as the bridge between Bao Dai and Ho Chih Minh. Both these men, it was felt, could easily step aside and allow the religionists to serve as the focus of all nationalists in Vietnam. Needless to say, neither the imperial throne nor the Communists were prepared to accede to the Cao Dai and Hoa Hao requests, nor to abandon their efforts to control the Vietnamese nation. This situation ended in 1954 with the fall of Dien Bien Phu and the partition of Vietnam.

At that time the Cao Dai and the Hoa Hao in effect came to terms with Ngo Dinh Diem. Since between them the two organizations controlled more than half the population of the southern delta, they were a political force of considerable significance. When Diem became premier of the new republic of South Vietnam in 1955, one of his first cabinets included four Cao Dai and four Hoa Hao ministers. Diem himself accepted this situation, however, only in order to rid himself of a chief of staff who was a Bao Dai appointee and supporter. Once having used the sects against Bao Dai — or indeed against the French generally, since imperial and French interests were linked — Diem then turned on the sects and disposed of them, attacking their armed units and arresting or buying out their leaders. By late 1955 or early 1956 the military formations of the Cao Dai and Hoa Hao were virtually destroyed. As a result the empires they had built after World War II in effect disappeared.

In the next period the harshness of the rule instituted by the Diem government led to a recrudescence of the Cao Dai and Hoa Hao organizations. There arose an agreement on the part of these bands that now began to re-form, if not to work directly with the National Liberation Front in South Vietnam, at least to enjoy the same type of relationship vis-à-vis the NLF that obtained in the earlier period when both forces were engaged in the struggle against the French. There developed a period of mutual toleration between the sects and the Viet Minh.

A kind of symbiotic relationship existed between the sects and the Communists from 1960 until November 1963, when Diem was overthrown. During this time, it seems clear on good authority, there was increasing Cao Dai and Hoa Hao opposition to the Diem government. As a result in virtually all the military regimes that succeeded Diem, there was in either the cabinet or the legislature some representation of the Cao Dai and Hoa Hao as political forces. Moreover, government tolerance of Cao Dai and Hoa Hao allowed a rebuilding of their shattered organizations, though this was not an easy process. The Cao Dai had lost repute because some of its generals had gone over to Diem, accepting bribes and betraying their followers. In addition after the death of pope Pham Cong Tac in 1959, there was no leadership capable of redirecting the Cao Dai organization. Cao Dai thus suffered inner dissension and declined.

Hoa Hao also experienced fragmentation. Following the death of Huynh Phu So, who was murdered by the Communists in April 1947, the organization broke up into a number of subsects. These groups were, however, far more dynamic than the Cao Dai and far more militant in their opposition to Diem and thus less susceptible of being bought out by him. As a result they maintained a much greater degree of cohesion and were in a better position to benefit from the overthrow of the Diem government in 1963.

Today the Hoa Hao in Vietnam is vigorous and active, appearing to possess great strength in the Mekong delta. In August 1967 Hoa Hao was operating four schools to train leaders and lay readers. It was interesting to observe the people attending these schools. Men and women ranging in age from 16 to 60 years sat with perfect discipline in large halls, listening intently to lectures, singing songs in unison, and responding collectively to questions put to them by the speaker. Observing these performances, one could easily understand the powerful effect which the sect and its ideology have had on the rural people. About 500 students were being trained in 1967 and about 2,000 in 1969. Wherever one goes in the delta areas where the sect is strong, one finds Hoa Hao reading halls and one also encounters, not far away, the political organization which is associated with the movement.

Thus the Hoa Hao and the Cao Dai share a similar history, both having gone through much the same evolution and both having emerged as major political forces. Both also have counterpart organizations which function as political parties. In September 1946 Huynh Phu So, the founder of the Hoa Hao, formed a Vietnam Democratic Socialist party, designed to regroup the resistance elements in South Vietnam which had come to disagree violently with the Viet Minh over problems of leadership. The party was described at the time as the union of a number of French-resisting political, religious, labor, and other groups, among them the former Vietnam National Independence party, the Cao Dai, and the Hoa Hao, and including as well various South Vietnamese intellectuals. The list of participating organizations is doubtless exaggerated but prominent individuals from them did in fact join the new party. Its principal leader had been a well-known spokesman for the Vietnam National Independence party. As long as Huynh Phu So was alive, the Vietnam Democratic Socialist party acted as the official political voice of the Hoa Hao movement. After his death in 1947 the party was partly divorced from the movement, although it was still considered a Hoa Hao organization; it was somewhat weakened too by a split between the Saigon organization and that located in the western parts of South Vietnam.

The program of the Vietnam Democratic Socialist party called for the independence of Vietnam; the establishment of a democratic regime in opposition to all forms of dictatorship; and the realization of a socialist society in which men would not exploit each other, in which everyone would have the right to compensation for his labor, and in which there would be, as might have been anticipated, no class struggle. The official paper was named *The Masses*. The party also endorsed the United Nations Organization and Vietnamese participation in it. Despite its religious base, it was similar to the Socialist International. This party, of course, suffered greatly at the hands of both the Viet Minh and Diem. In fact, one of its prominent leaders, who had helped Diem in 1955, was later executed by the Diem government. When one talks to members of the organization, it becomes clear that they possess a vivid recollection of their sufferings at the hands of both the Communists and the Diem dictatorship.

The political counterpart of Cao Dai was the Vietnam Restoration Association, which tried at one point to form a Cao Dai League. This organization, directed by the pope of the order, carried on some political activities, or at least offered a political vehicle for such activities.

The Roman Catholics. The third movement, one which need be treated only briefly, is that of the Catholics. It may suffice to note that they are strong, well organized, and claim 1,800,000 adherents, although this figure may be slightly exaggerated. Their groups are organized as are Catholic churches everywhere; they consist of parish organizations as well as various orders, and are administered by native members of the hierarchy. The Catholics are to be found in the military, in the civil service, and in business and the professions. They represent the urbanized middle class in Vietnam from the north, center, and south. More than half of them are people who emigrated to the south, and they, along with the urban middle classes of the south itself, are the most westernized sector of the Vietnamese population. Because of their connections with the Catholic hierarchy, the development of prestige arising from membership in the Catholic church, and the advantages of Catholic higher education, they have come to be the best organized politically of the current groups in Vietnam.

The Buddhists. Of greater interest, because of its more indigenous origins, is the development of Buddhist reform movements in the 1930s. These movements established "studies associations" in Saigon in 1931, in Hué in 1932, and in Hanoi in 1934. The movements tended to prosper only in central Vietnam, where a newly founded Buddhist seminary at Hué became the center of a group of young reform-minded Buddhists. The young monks were taught to create in Vietnam the equivalent of the sangha, the extremely strong hierarchical Buddhist organization that has developed in Ceylon, Burma, Thailand, and other Theravada lands. The Vietnamese movement was not, however, Theravadist but essentially Mahayanist in its doctrine and approach. Virtually all Buddhists who have achieved prominence in the political struggles of Vietnam either attended the seminary in the 1930s or were taught by those trained there.

One of the groups created by the monks was the Annam Buddhist Studies Association. This organization was deliberately designed to renew the traditional culture; it was not a syncretistic form of Buddhism like Cao Dai or Hoa Hao. In mobilizing traditional culture against the West (i.e., France) reform Buddhists sought to assert their nationalism by revitalizing the faith of their ancestors. They prospered precisely at the times when French authority became weak and when there were periods of crisis.

In 1951 a Buddhist Association Congress united northern Buddhists who had emigrated to the south with the central and southern Buddhist groups. The result has been a generally increasing unity of Buddhists, all coming into the General Buddhist Association. The general association includes even the subsects of the Hoa Hao, though not the Cao Dai, which is not recognized as a Buddhist group. The unified Buddhist congregation which developed had, as one of its major associations, the Institute for the Execution of the Dharma (Buddhist law). This institute (in Vietnamese *Dien Hoa Dau*) is the political, secular arm of the unified Buddhist congregation; it has engaged in all the political struggles in Vietnam, beginning with the overthrow of Diem and including later actions directed against the subsequent military governments.

The Buddhist organizations are not, however, united in terms of their political objectives, with the exception of the unit led by the well-known Thich Tri Quang. The Buddhist groups that exist in the Saigon area are divided in their purposes, and there are also Theravada Buddhist organizations, which do not share the militant views held by members of the *Dien Hoa Dau*. Only in central Vietnam has there been an effective Buddhist movement, a reflection of the important role played by Thich Tri Quang. His organization divided all of Vietnam into eight regions, equivalent to dioceses, and has attempted to structure an organization down to the grass roots in order to develop a furthering of tradition. This structural device, developed in connection with Buddhist Congress meetings in Ceylon, India, Burma, and Thailand, was a deliberate effort to copy an organizational form which had not previously existed in Vietnam and by means of it to create a strong Buddhist movement.

The Sectarian Role in Vietnamese Politics. Each of the major religious groupings in modern South Vietnam can to some degree be evaluated by its strength in the senate and the house of representatives. While the proportions of representation change with each election, it appears that the Roman Catholic and the Buddhist groups are continuing elements of importance in the governmental organization, eclipsing to some extent the other sects. Actually, the recent senate membership is not proportional to the local and regional importance of the respective religious groupings. The South Vietnamese house of representatives is far more representative because its members are chosen from local districts. Of the 137 members in 1968, there were 46 Buddhists, 35 Catholics, 13 Hoa Hao, and 5 Cao Dai, as well as representatives of other ethnic and religious minorities. These figures convey some idea of the relative strength of the religious groups in Vietnamese politics.

Catholics, Hoa Hao, Cao Dai, and Buddhists, in any combination, can if they wish create tremendous problems for the South Vietnamese government. At the present time many provincial and district chiefs, members of the popular and regional forces, and even entire units of the South Vietnamese army are either Hoa Hao or Cao Dai. This means that they have effective control of the areas where they are dominant. In the countryside these two groups combined can muster support from at least half the population of the delta areas of South Vietnam. The Buddhists and the Catholics, because of their high visibility and importance in Saigon and in central Vietnam — the Buddhists, despite the losses they have suffered, still possess the bulk of the support of the people — can also play an important role in the government's struggle against its Communist competition in South Vietnam. In the past Catholic and Buddhist demonstrations have been able to bring down governments. Should either of these two major groups be antagonized in some way by the present regime, it is quite likely that the government will in short order find itself in a political crisis.

In South Vietnam a major role is played by these various religious groups in determining the strength, the structure, and the future outcome of the country. Whether the war ends through negotiation or as a result of military victory by one side or the other, the fact remains that these four major religious groupings are strong, well-organized, and amply supported by the organic village unit; any political organization or any effective combination of organizations in Vietnam must take them into account.

} AGEHANANDA BHARATI {

Hinduism and Modernization

In any discussion of the modernization of religious forces of Hinduism, today's intellectual in India is likely to express a number of distinct views. The individual born in South Asia who speaks an Indian language but who prefers to converse in English will insist that Hinduism is a "way of life" rather than a series of specific practices. Whatever it may be, however, he will maintain that it cannot conflict with the world of today. By its very nature Hinduism is held to be "scientific," in no way reflecting the Christian or Muslim tendency toward medieval or antimodernistic dogma. It is fair to state that this opinion is shared by virtually all Westernized, articulate Indians, although perhaps the few who are trained in the social sciences of the West or in literary criticism would take exception to it.

The modernization of Hinduism can be discussed from two primary viewpoints, both of which are intrinsic to Hinduism. Neither can be separated from the other without the intensive kind of analysis that is undertaken by an anthropologist. The two viewpoints are applicable to all traditional systems of Hinduism and consist of the doctrinal, theological, and ideological, as against the pragmatic, social, and operational aspects of Hinduism.

But it is apparent that the stage must be set before a discussion of the precise aspects of modernization can begin. This is true because the Indian intellectual of today, seeking to convince any public he addresses of the scientific nature of Hinduism, has developed a special parlance, a distinctive style of communication, crucial to the analysis of "modernization." Modern anthropology has of late developed a strong concern with the ethnography of communication (cf., e.g., Hymes, 1964; Gumperz, 1964). The way in which a person refers to any topic derives, it is clear, from the orientation to the topic which he brings from his background and culture. This special parlance is then relevant to the interpretation which an anthropologist or, indeed, any behavioral scientist makes of cultural and behavioral circumstances.

In respect to the modern Indian or, more precisely, to the modern Indian apologist, the manner in which he handles his dialogue provides a wealth of instances from which ethnolinguistic inferences can be drawn. Indeed if one were to go even farther and tabulate everything that modern Indians say about their own culture and religion, it might be possible to define a concept of modernization in its dialectic aspect. Or, to put the matter more simply, when a reference is made to Hinduism and modernization, it may suffice to analyze, anthropologically and philosophically, what the modern Indians *say*.

One further preliminary is necessary — a consideration of certain terminological classifications. For the past three decades, both Indian and Western social scientists have been making use of such terms as the "Great Tradition" versus the "Little Tradition," as well as Hinduization, Sanskritization, Westernization, modernization, parochialism, or, indeed, parochialization as against universalization. But whatever the term, the implication is always one of contrast and interaction between units of greater and lesser magnitude. On the one hand there is the village, the community in isolation, with its particular sets of beliefs and customs; on the other there is the impact of the deeply rooted historical tradition, the civilization and its ethos.

In order to report cultural change on the Indian subcontinent, this writer has suggested elsewhere some modifications in the use of the concepts of "Great" and "Little Tradition" (Bharati, 1968). These terms, even in the way they have been used by such writers as Srivinas (1952), Redfield and Singer (1954), and the University of Chicago school in general, have utility and a considerable heuristic value — if, of course, they are not overworked. Professor Singer's approach to the Great versus Little Tradition concept is useful in providing categories for an evaluation of both religious and secular behavior in India in a period of rapid social change and transition. On an incipient level of analysis, these catchall terms are thus helpful in separating two operationally disparate issues.

But there is also the concept of a Renaissance which seems to elude either category of this terminology. This is implicit in the notion of Hinduization, a process whereby local populations or ethnic groups of the subcontinent, those possessing a tribal background, may assume the ways of their more respected Hindu neighbors, absorbing so much of the Hindu customs that their tribal lore becomes a part of local or regional Hindu lore. The processes involved are effectively stereotyped. There is a progression from the tribal to the Hinduized way of life, following a pattern both predictable and essentially current in South Asia.

Sanskritization, on the other hand, is a much more complex phenomenon (Stahl, 1963; Gould, 1962). It does not imply the study of Sanskrit or even its ritualistic use. The process is unique to India and has no parallel elsewhere in the world. When people in South Asia "modernize," they can enter into any phase of technological innovation provided they have undergone the process of Sanskritization. Involved is the adherence to certain forms of traditional behavior epitomized in the Sanskrit language, its hieratic literature, and the centuries-old practices associated with it. Whenever a group seeks to become more highly respected by its Hindu neighbors of higher caste status, it assumes Sanskritic rituals identifiable through acts both of commission and omission, as the case may be, and founded on the sacerdotal, Sanskritic tradition — on the patterns, in short, related to the acts of Brahmins (Cohn, 1959).

A simple example of this process may be seen in a caste of tanners in South India. If such a group seeks to become more acceptable and respectable in the eyes of the surrounding Hindus, its leaders must decree, and succeed in implementing, the omission of those occupational and ritual acts which in the wider Hindu context are regarded as defiling. Involved might be a decree which prohibits the remarriage of widows, for example, or a change in diet patterns, such as those relating to the consumption of meat and especially of carrion beef, or a change in the worship of those deities which lack an ideological link with the pantheon of Sanskritic divinities. Literally hundreds of tribal and other low caste groups have not traditionally employed Brahmin priests for their ceremonies at marriage and funerals, but in the process of their modernization they have gone through a phase of Sanskritization, meaning the acceptance of the Brahmin and his rituals as instrumental in the performance of rites of passage and other ceremonial observances.

There is a recent exception to this general rule, one resting on a kind of inverse Sanskritization. The *Dravida Kazhagam* and the *Munnetra Kazhagam* of Tamilnad reject any connection with the Sanskrit cultural base. Gods with Hindu names are not accepted and the images of such Sanskritic gods as Ganesha are carried in procession and incinerated. Sanskrit loanwords are rather laboriously replaced in ritual by Dravidian words and their compounds. Yet even this process derives its inspiration from a model — there is a standard literary configuration at the base of such induced culture change. In all other parts of India Sanskrit remains the pattern; it is only in the highly politicized Tamilian south where Tamil and Dravidian form the teleological matrix.

Some authors have used the terms "modernization" and "Westernization" interchangeably in the Indian context. This seems generally justifiable but it reflects a question of emphasis rather than one of content. Technological and kindred phenomena of change may conveniently be termed those of "modernization," while the term "Westernization" may be reserved to treat processes of ideological and discursive or dialectic diffusion from non-indigenous sources.

As these various terminological issues are reviewed, it appears that the contrast between the Great Tradition and the Little Tradition still retains utility. It is true that some controversy has arisen about the use of the terms, especially among Indologists. But, as has recently been suggested (Bharati, 1968), they provide a viable taxonomic and heuristic device, applicable not only to South Asia but to other literate and agricultural societies as well. While Singer (1966) has applied them most directly to the contemporary Hindu scene, they seem equally applicable to any society which possesses both an oral and a written corpus of canonical and other traditional themes. The Great Tradition in China, for example, implies Confucian literature and exegesis, perhaps embellished by Taoist and Buddhist intrusions. What people in Chinese villages do, how they apply Confucian, Taoist, or Buddhist elements to their daily lives and attitudes, to their interpretations of the familial cult or ancestral reverence, are factors and elements of the Little Tradition. And the same distinction can be made with respect to India.

One need only think, for example, of the village priest or the wandering mendicant (*sādhu, vairāgī, sannyāsī*). Both have a fairly thorough idea of the literary lore and of all those elements in the Hindu tradition which might be classified as pertinent to a Great Tradition. A *purohita* (full-time priestly practitioner) knows the titles of the scriptures, can quote more or less fluently from appropriate passages in them, can identify the *gotra** of his clients, and can pronounce in general terms on the philosophy and ideology underlying Hinduism. Villagers may worship one or many gods, most of whom are no doubt of purely local or regional origin. Some of these village gods are Sanskrit divinities in disguise — or so, at least, the *purohita* may declare — that is, deities of the

* A *gotra* is a patrisib with a mythical founder at its apex, usually a *rsi* or seer who recorded and reported a branch of the Veda. The *gotra* is an exogamous unit; women assume their husband's *gotra* on marriage; the *gotra* cuts across religious lines: Muslims and Jains as well as Christians have *gotras* due to their Hindu ancestry.

Vedic or later mythological pantheon. But most of the village deities, demigods, demons, sprites, and spirits would have to be regarded as purely local were it not for the intriguing all-Indian tendency to interpret even the most minor deity of the Little Tradition in terms of the Great Tradition. Godling X of Village 1 is thus said to be a manifestation of the Lord Siva; Goddess Y of Locality 2 is a form of the Sanskritic mother-goddess Ambā, Umā, Durga, Pārvatī, or any other.

Over a long period of time the Indian has come to realize that his *dih* is none other than the great Vedic god or goddess. To the outsider it appears that the villager tends to camouflage the local aspect of his worship and his pantheon, according them a Sanskritized veneer. In a village in Bengal, for example, a mother-goddess is encountered everywhere, a divinity charged with diagnosing, preventing, or healing smallpox, rinderpest, or snakebite. This is the grass-roots divinity. Yet when the villager deals with his deities in a situation involving the external world, such a goddess is invariably identified with Durga or Kali, the partly Sanskritic divinity of Bengal. To the field anthropologist these are Little Tradition gods viewed as part of a village as an isolate. Nevertheless a transition has been made when Great Tradition parlance is used to explain village divinities as manifestations of Vedic and post-Vedic gods, not only Indra and Varuna, among other names invoked in the Great Tradition ritual, but also the supreme divinities of latter-day popular Hinduism, Siva, Vishnu, or Ganesha.

There is no conflict here, but the point does emerge that Westernization and modernization cannot be viewed interchangeably. It is obvious that the contemporary Indian villager's tendency to explain his local god as a Vedic figure cannot possibly be termed an aspect of Westernization. And yet it is perhaps one of the most prominent features of modernization, arising where Sanskritization is one of the more striking aspects of the overall process of culture change.

The native apologist for modern India, the Indian intellectual in Shils's sense (cf. 1961), is not inclined to admit that modernization in India presupposes a temporary phase of Sanskritization.

The modern Indian — the man who speaks English, however poorly, and who prefers the English All-India radio program to the vernacular — belongs to a sociocultural milieu which has carried Sanskritization with it from its own past. In other words, Indian students, travelers, scholars, journalists, or politicians have themselves been raised in an atmosphere of Sanskritization. They and their parents, together with their children who now "run" India, are part of this Renaissance. Even if it be assumed that the majority of them are not interested in religion as such, as they might say of themselves, all are Sanskritized people. Those who do not represent this orientation — those in insular areas where Sanskritization has not made an impact — do not represent modern India anywhere. It is also true that many modern Indians prefer not to be reminded of the process and its role; some who do admit it may reject and censure it, calling it superstitious and regrettable.

The Great and Little Traditions have thus lived side by side for many centuries. They do so at the grass-roots level in South Asia today. Yet modernization in the manner in which modern Indians understand it does not touch this level at all. Indians and their non-Indian admirers may raise questions as to whether people in India *really* follow this model; or whether they will not accept new technology, new irrigation methods and fertilizers, or a more up-to-date market and banking system, without first undergoing the process of Sanskritization. But such objections are not germane to our inquiry. There are nuclear physicists of Brahmin stock who have remained strict vegetarians and who perform *pūjā* (formal worship) and *sandhyā* (minimal Vedic observances incumbent on "twice-born" Hindus) every morning and evening; there are many others who eat beef and drink Scotch, and relish both. But again this has nothing to do with the pervasive process being analyzed here, which operates on a more sophisticated and intensive level than modern Indians can possibly appreciate. The Little Traditions of the Indian village proper have not changed or "modernized" themselves; whatever changes they have undergone were changes toward greater Sanskritization. The Little Traditions of the village could not be modified without breaking down the fabric and the structure of the village commune. When contemporary Hinduism in the village is studied, i.e., at its grass-roots level, no change can be seen except in terms of Sanskritization. There does not seem to be any other means of analysis. This is not a logical or a categorical claim; it is simply a statement of a very intricate set of empirical observations shared by the best anthropological minds of India and the West, one arising over a period of four decades or more.

The terms Hinduization and Sanskritization no doubt worry those who do not see Hinduism or the Sanskritic lore in its many guises and disguises. Villagers and tribals, after all, have been converted to non-Hindu and non-Sanskrit religions, to Islam and to various forms of Christianity. Yet strangely, even where the official change is one toward an ostensibly different ideological or doctrinal set, Hinduization and Sanskritization have been at work, and not even just subtly. Whether a village becomes Hindu, Muslim, or Christian, the hierarchy of defilement and purity persists. Those who eat meat will be less respected and will, in the long run, have a lower ritualistic status than those who do not, those who consume alcohol will have lesser status than those who do not, and the Christian or Islamic rules about these matters are only the overt basis for an evaluation which uses the covert Hindu referential orientation.

India's Great Tradition — its ideas, its fictions, its assumptions, and its parlance — prevails as Indians modernize, whether as groups or as individuals. The new identities as Hindus, Muslims, Christians, or "Indians" are therefore not significantly important.

This approach to the study of modern India, including the cities and the English-speaking elite, is constantly vitiated by the limitations which anthropologists and Indologists have set themselves. Indian philosophers today, i.e., people who teach philosophy, Eastern and Western, at Indian colleges, have been fascinated by eighteenth- and nineteenth-century European philosophy, particularly by system-building and dialectic. In their apologetics relating to Indian philosophy, they espouse the European writers whose ideas seem to be similar to those of the official reformed Hinduism. Modern Indian philosophers delight in such relatively unknown British and continental authors as Bosanquet, Pringle-Pattison, Haeckel, Bradley, and, inevitably, Hegel, whose pompous forensic seems to be the *summum bonum* to many Indian teachers of philosophy. In fact when professional Indian philosophers speak about "modern thought," they are inclined to refer to Hegel and his European contemporaries. Eminent scholars like T. R. V. Murti have used the Hegelian stance to present Indian thought to the West. In his *Central Philosophy of Buddhism* (1955) Murti seems to aver that a Hegelian interpretation of Indian thought bestows some special merit on it; he does not see that such attempts at vindication do more harm than good to the Indian philosophical image. The reason Karl H. Potter's excellent study (1963) is unpopular among Indian teachers of philosophy is precisely his implicit rejection of nineteenth-century European systematic philosophy and its replacement by more genuinely modern analytical and logical tools.

There is little knowledge of and less sympathy for ordinary language philosophy or the analytic thought of contemporary British and American philosophers. This writer, with his former colleague J. L. Mehta, director of the Institute of Advanced Philosophical Research at Banaras Hindu University, bootlegged A. J. Ayer, G. Ryle, and Wittgenstein into the postgraduate philosophy curriculum at that school by using considerable diplomatic skill and a few administrative ruses. The anthropologist reporting on India may conclude that modern Indian utterances are best analyzed by the methods of ordinary language philosophy.* This type of analysis does not halt before profound statements, it is not impressed by the sanctimoniousness of metaphysical and intuitive

---

* This is a narrower group of philosophers than the logical positivists, logical (scientific) empiricists, or analytic philosophers. The main British writers in ordinary language philosophy are J. L. Austin, Stuart Hampshire, R. M. Hare, and S. Toulmin; among the growing number of American ordinary language thinkers, two young scholars are outstanding, P. Butchvarov and A. R. Louch. Roughly 20 percent of all British and American philosophy department faculty are directly identifiable with ordinary language philosophy.

pronouncements, nor of course by the redemptory underpinnings of Indian philosophical jargon. The dry, clear, emotionally relentless, and ideologically uncompromising style of analytic philosophy no doubt annoys the modern Indian thinker, not only because of its seemingly disrespectful style but also because it makes short shrift of claims of intuitive profundity. More importantly, however, it cuts through the modern Indian's statements about his own society. It can be demonstrated that an ordinary language method helps to appraise Indian utterances about India's modernization. This method can also be used to analyze Hindu and Buddhist heterodox literature and religious practice (Bharati, 1966).

There are basically two kinds of scholars reporting on India. The Indologist and the cultural anthropologist are two very different creatures, though recent developments have proved that they can meet and combine in a single person — unthinkable until a decade ago. The Indologists talked about what Indians wrote and talked about. The anthropologist talks about Indian society as it is today — not as the modern Indian wants it to be, but as it is. Indologists are not concerned with the operation of Indian society. Indian-born Indologists of course know more about their society than do their Western colleagues, simply because they happen to have been born into it. Yet when speaking about Indian society, including the problems of modernization, Indian-born Indologists are not much less naïve than their Western colleagues. At meetings of the American Oriental Society or at such conventions as the International Congress of Orientalists held at Ann Arbor in 1967, the anthropologist is baffled by the incredible ignorance displayed by the most erudite among the interpreters of Indian literature, Sanskrit, Prakrit, and others. Knowledge of Vedānta, Navya-Nyāya, or Buddhist epistemology does not provide any clue to the operation of Indian society, not even of the period when those systems of thought were conceived and promulgated. Yet the orientalist believes that he does know the essence of Indian society, whatever that means, and that he can explain modernization by referring to the familiar corpus of ancient lore. No doubt the cultural anthropologist tends to be equally naïve when it comes to India's Great Tradition lore, and his gullibility vis-à-vis the Indian informant who represents that tradition is perhaps equally embarrassing. Since these two fields of investigation are no more connected than, say, Aquinas' *Summa contra Gentiles* with gun salutes and apple pie on Memorial Day, the Indologist and the anthropologist have to merge, in one fashion or another, when they want to report on patterns that include both the written tradition and the workings of Indian society. Modernization in Hinduism is precisely such a pattern.

In the light of these preliminaries, then, we can turn to an analysis of the modernization of Hinduism first as doctrine and second as a social or cultural phenomenon (cf. Opler, 1944). The question may arise as to the existence of an operational bridge between the two. A corpus of utterances by modern Hindus about Hindu doctrine and its evaluation cuts across both sections, since this corpus, when analyzed, is such an operational connector and since doctrine per se is what Indologists are concerned about. But what people do is what the ethnologist tries to present. And what people *say* about the doctrine is very much part of what they *do*, especially when action terms are used in the context provided by such analytic philosophers of ordinary language as Ryle, J. L. Austin, and Stuart Hampshire. In this manner overlap is eliminated. The doctrine as written and handed down in the grass-roots tradition of oral and literary orthodoxy (*paramparā*) stands at one end of the Indologist-anthropologist continuum; it is subject matter for the Indologist. The actions of the modern Indian in his society, his interactions with people and with thoughts extraneous to his society, are studied by the ethnologist. The cultural anthropologist, studying modernization, evaluates actual statements by actual people about their tradition, and the structure of modernization can be gleaned from the manner in which this corpus deviates from the traditional doctrine.

Modern Indians use culture-relating language in two different ways. This no doubt reflects the ambivalent linguistic and nonlinguistic behavior which has struck Western observers. The Indian who travels in India or abroad has a Great Tradition to fall back on when challenged by external, even if not necessarily hostile, parlance. He has, however, lost his rural roots and his attempt to be a modern Hindu and a Westerner at the same time is fraught with linguistic and behavioral conflicts. This reinforces the contention that studying modern Hinduism means listening to Hindus talk about it as an apologetic of a tradition which they partly reject and which they partly modify in order to make it conform with their notions of modern thought and dialogue.

The speeches and writings of Swami Vivekānanda, Śrī Aurobindo, Swami Śivānanda, and more recently Maharishi Mahesh Yogi — not to mention an impressive number of monastics of every shade of naïveté and sophistication — are the corpus of modern Hinduism. This corpus lies not in the scriptures to which they obliquely refer, nor in the frequent and perfunctory quotations of certain stereotyped scriptural verses, although the swamis and lay spokesmen of modernized Hinduism include large and crucial chunks of actual Hindu doctrine in their utterances. But it would appear that the modern Hindu excludes those elements of the written lore which complicate a very simplistic world view. The modern Hindu who thinks in English or in a vernacular that has translated an English sermon into its idiom, wants to speak about Vedānta, about *bhakti*, perhaps about *yoga*; but he does not want to be quizzed nor hear about Sāmkhya, Nyāya, Vaiśesika, or about ritualism. As long as he can get away with it, the modern Hindu wants to declare Hindu doctrine as something not really different from Christian or any other religious teaching. On the sociological side he will deny the existence of caste and, again if he can get away with it, he will declare that "caste has been abolished." This cannot even be said in an Indian language — it would make no sense at all. Thus the frequently heard English-language utterance "caste has been abolished," if translated into any Indian language, would mean something like "the social structure has been abolished," which is patent nonsense.

On the doctrinal side the modern Hindu defines his religious creed by quoting those portions of the scripture which have been cathected by the founders of the Renaissance. Swami Vivekānanda said that it was more important for young Bengalis to play a game of football (meaning soccer, of course) than to read the *Bhagavadgītā.* "The Bhagavadgītā teaches the quintessence of all religions," the late Dr. Bhagavan Dass wrote; "mind control is man control" — Swami Śivānanda; "the difference between India and the West is that India is spiritual, the West is materialistic." The literature representing the Hindu Renaissance and its apologetics is vast and growing. Pamphlets, little books, large volumes, journals, in English and in all the Indian languages, appeal to modern Hindus. All these writings are conscious or unintended imitations of the words and works of Swami Vivekānanda. Simplistic moral exhortation, with constant stress on the virtue of chastity *(brahmacaryam)*, mind control, love of all beings, the viewing of all as the same *(samadrsti)*, belong to the permanent repertory of the modern apologetic genre.

Perhaps an even more important feature of the modernization of Hinduism is its boundless eclecticism. This quality is epitomized by the undue favor given to the *Bhagavadgītā* (notwithstanding Vivekānanda's *obiter dictum,* quoted above, which was due to overcompensation, or, more simply, to the syndrome of the lady protesting too much). An important text no doubt even in classical India, the *Bhagavadgītā* is, however, a noncanonical work. It is not a theologically sophisticated or speculatively profound text. Set as a pep talk given by Krishna to his hesitant friend, the attraction of the *Bhagavadgītā* for modern Hindus seems to lie in its own doctrinal eclecticism. It combines elements from the quietistic Upanisads, from the more activist lore of the Purānas and earlier Epics, as well as the excitement engendered by the fact that the speaker uses a situationally fascinating setting for his instruction — a situation with which people in all critical situations can identify. Bhagavan Dass, a truly erudite man, gave ample praise to the *Gītā,* and his own work reflects the hypertrophic eclecticism of the Renaissance. Everything is acceptable, and differences of a doctrinal or ideological sort have to be underplayed or ignored.* This eclecticism relates to the more general outlook of Hindus toward the modern encounter. Obviously, if India is to rank on a par with the technologically advanced nations, its autochthonous doctrines should not only tolerate teachings stemming from other regions, but should not be radically different from them. Gods and rituals, complex ceremonials, the multiplicity of denomination, all this is not the sort of thing a modern man should accept. What is needed, indeed, is a simple monotheism joined with a sort of Protestant ethic, preferably but not necessarily associated with Sanskrit terms.

There is a weak parallel to this in America. The Unitarian Church has apparently been quite successful in eliminating all theological features that might make it unacceptable to anyone. The same thing is happening to modernized urban Hinduism. What does the modern Hindu mean when he says that India is spiritual and that this contrasts with the materialism of the West? Taken at its face value, the proposition is nonsense. All students of urban India know that affluent Indians, *marvārīs*, and other businessmen and industrialists, as well as the *nouveau riche*, seek eagerly for the gadgets which are the hallmark of "materialism." Modern Indian homes of some affluence are full of chintz and kitsch, and one often gets the impression that the quantity of items kept in the living room is intended to document wealth.

The Indian student of medicine or chemical engineering who utters the "spiritual-materialistic" cliché echoes the belief of Swami Vivekānanda and the early fathers of modern Hinduism that the West is more given to material values than India. More perspicacious Hindu scholars have pointed to the absurdity of this wellnigh universal Indian assumption (R. Iyer, 1965). There is little doubt, however, that the people of South Asia, whatever their social and economic trappings, place greater emphasis on theological matters, on religious discourse, and on all the corollaries of the

* The political orientation in nationalist India has much to do with this. By constitutional ascription, India is a secular state; all religions are equal, hence differences must not be important. The causes for the denial of important differences lie much deeper and are beyond the scope of this essay.

transcendental than the average Western man. But this quality
of spirituality is precisely what the modern Indian wants to deny,
for he tries to make outsiders believe that all these "superstitions"
have been forgotten and that modern Hindus believe in a simple,
secular type of Hinduism. He insists that this type of Hinduism
makes India more spiritual, not realizing its resemblance to a similar kind of Protestantism in the West — a not-too-demanding,
Sunday-type conformity which deemphasizes the two primary nu-
clei of the religious life, theology and mystical involvement. If one
interviews a *kuli* at Calcutta or a farmer behind his plow in Bihar
about his views of *karma*, rebirth, the powers of the gods, their relation to the Universal Being, and other matters of theological import, these men will offer a simple, but not incorrect statement of
the theological situation. They will not turn away, saying they are
not interested in such matters. The village Hindu, not touched by
modernism and the Renaissance, has a far more coherent and complex theological view than the hypertrophically eclectic modern
Hindu in the city. It is the village Hindu who is more conversant
with religious matters than is the Christian in the West.

In differing degrees of sophistication, the English-speaking modern will draw upon such sources as Vivekānanda, Śivānanda, Aurobindo, Dayānanda, and the Arya Samāj preachments, depending
on his regional background and on his formal education. People
who have read eighteenth- and nineteenth-century British poetry
in college tend to espouse Aurobindo, whose creations have an un-
canny resemblance to some, though not to the best, of Victorian
writing. But this again has hardly any parallel in the Western
world. Talk of theology is no longer carried on in American
churches, which have become congregations for properly functioning social dialogue and conformity. Modern Christian theologians
like Tillich, Wach, or Bultmann are philosophers and scholars who
appeal to a learned or a very select lay audience. This, however,
does not mean that the American or European public is therefore
less "spiritual" or more "materialistic" in the sense of being more
comfort-oriented *in principle*, as modern Indians aver. The dis-
parity here is of a much cruder kind; Americans can obtain gadg-

ets freely and cheaply because they earn what it takes to buy them — hence the more sophisticated among them begin to feel embarrassed about comfort-producing gadgetry, a feeling modern Indians would like to have.

Few modern Indians can dispense with their fascination for the gadget — Nehru overtly admitted it. It may well be that because the West has what modern Indians would like to possess —namely, gadgets and the machine tools to make them, as well as the money to buy them — the Renaissance Indian transfers his fascination to the producers of the objects of fascination. Hence the continuing charge that the West is materialistic. Those Indians who can afford to buy gadgets, do it, proudly and eagerly. The late M. N. Roy distinguished between "vulgar materialism," meaning the display of gadgetry among the wealthy minority on the subcontinent, and refined materialism as an ideology, propounded in India only, alas, by the unknown and cryptic teacher Cārvāka of early days, and by modern Western thinkers and their Eastern disciples. But an analysis of the content of the materialistic side of Indian philosophy shows that there is really more philosophical materialism in the Indian tradition of thought than is true in the West (Riepe, 1961).

A summary of the modifications which traditional Hinduism as doctrine has undergone in the process of modernization offers five points:

1. Initially, there are the stylistic trends, the spelling rules, so to speak, of modern Hinduism. These are completely eclectic. The more knowledgeable spokesmen of the Hindu Renaissance, like the late Śrī Aurobindo and the Pondicherry-centered cult with its national and international clientele, would stand at the upper end of the scale, and the style of Swami Śivānanda and the scores of small aśramite institutions with their monastic leadership would stand at the lower end, with a variety of more or less literate, proselytizing agents in between. The better-read apologist, i.e., the man who has had some formal religious reading or instruction, adduces the rule of *samanvaya* to justify his eclecticism. However,

the term has been misunderstood even by men of considerable learning such as Bhagavan Dass.

Samanvaya is a traditional though not canonical injunction for pandits to find a basic agreement among themselves in the process of *śāstrārtha* (learned discussion on religious exegesis in Sanskrit), despite the varying persuasions and arguments in their respective interpretations. The traditional pandits tried to arrive at a solution that would be at least formally acceptable to all concerned; the minimal criterion was that a door should be left open for further dialogue. But *samanvaya* never meant what the more learned modern eclectics think it did. It did not include Islam, Christianity, Buddhism, communism, nationalism, or "science," nor even the quasi secularism of the modern political jargon. *Samanvaya* applies only to participants in the Brahmin tradition that accepts *śruti* as epistemological proof, on a par with direct perception and inference. Consensus about the Vedic authority as supreme and undisputable was the universal premise in all applications of *samanvaya*, and remains so even now when grass-roots theologians get together. It certainly did not apply to Buddhism or Jainism or to anyone who was called a *nāstika* (the term "agnostic" or "unbeliever" is a bad translation, frequently found in texts written by modern authors). *Nāstiko vedanindakah* — "He who denies (the authority of) the Veda is a *nāstika*" — and *samanvaya* does not apply to him even if he is well versed and admittedly superior in the art of theological dispute. It is also quite irrelevant whether a man believes in God. What makes him a Hindu, and what makes his disquisitions come within the ken of *samanvaya*, is his acceptance of *śruti* as epistemological proof on a level with other incontrovertible means of proof, a very different thing from the Christian or even the Islamic concept of "faith." Typically a modern Hindu would say that Hinduism is all-tolerant, that it embraces every religion. But *samanvaya* is something quite different, and those scholars within the Renaissance who know about *samanvaya* consistently confuse it with "tolerance" in order to legitimize their universalistic claims.

2. Modernized Hinduism as most comprehensively propounded

by Vivekānanda differs from traditional doctrines and interpretations in its claim that everybody is right, theologically speaking. There is a modern claim to complete tolerance in Hinduism, a powerful and highly suggestive tool in the modern Hindu's dispute with Western, especially Christian, speakers. All Hindus would claim that Hinduism is tolerant, that it does not denigrate other religions. Modern Hindus, with the exception of those who are professional practitioners of the tradition, tend to be highly resilient and one hears statements to the effect that anybody who believes in God is a Hindu, or that anybody who does good is a Hindu, or that anybody who performs the proper social actions is a Hindu. The writer has often encountered strong opposition among modern Hindus when he stated that a Hindu is identified first by his birth and second by his acceptance of the *śruti* as authority. The traditional notion is refuted by such statements as "this is narrow-minded," "this is superstition," "these are the old-fashioned ideas we should abandon."

In comparison to the more fundamentalistic orientations of Islam and Christianity, Hinduism in any of its forms is of course more tolerant. However, tolerance comes to an abrupt end when pandits and other specialists who identify with a specific scholastic tradition within Hinduism sit in dispute. There is no tolerance at all between, say, the Madhavite Vaisnava and the Śamkarite monist; nor is there much tolerance between Hindu scholars and Buddhist savants whenever they get together for the purpose of *śāstrārtha*, i.e., serious discussion of religious texts and issues — something that has not happened for over a thousand years, but that now has begun to occur sporadically in Asian circles concerned with ideological resuscitation. The convert Buddhist Mahārs in Central India, for example, have invited Buddhist monks and Hindu *sannyāsis* and Brahmins to discuss religious issues.

3. Somewhat esoteric to the non-Indologist, but crucial to the understanding of modern Hindu doctrine, is the systematic, even though partly unconscious, suppression of the traditional distinction between *śruti* and *smrti*. *Śruti* is the name for the corpus of canonical texts the acceptance of which is incumbent upon the

Hindu. One may interpret *śruti* as one pleases, but as a Hindu one cannot deny its authority.* All other texts, the Epics including the *Bhagavadgītā*, the Purānas, and the various *sūtras* are *smrti* ("that which is to be remembered") and the Hindu is free to accept or reject their tenets. The dialectic stance has been to accept *smrti* unless a clash is seen with any *śruti* statement. *Śruti*, literally, "that which is heard," implies "that which has to be heard, i.e., accepted." But what is so important in this context is the fact that the *Bhagavadgītā* has tacitly been given *śruti* status. Very few modern English-speaking Hindus who know the difference ever speak about it; all of them, including Gandhi and the political leaders of modern Hindu India, have believed that this text is the "Bible" of Hinduism, and that it contains the essentials of the Hindu creed. It is, however, nothing of the sort. The *Bhagavadgītā* teaches activity in society and the struggle for justice or patriotism. Quite naturally the modern Indian wants to see an important aspect of modern life supported by the text. The fact that the *Bhagavadgītā* has indeed become the focal primary text of the Renaissance is due precisely to this confusion; its attractive eclecticism accounts for its rise in status.

The *Gītā* contains, as all Sanskritists know, a blend of many conflicting traditions and contradictory teachings. But the activistic elements in it make the text highly eligible as a code for the founders of Indian nationalism, and — as must be clear by now — the interaction of the nationalists with the religious leaders of the Renaissance is constant and incisive. Somehow the leaders of modern India entertain the notion that nationalism, democracy, and even socialism and communism are or could be interpretations of injunctions given in the *Bhagavadgītā*. Swami Avyaktānanda, former head of the Ramakrishna Mission Center in London, pro-

* In fact the minimum definition of a Hindu, apart from his descent from a Hindu family, is precisely his acceptance of the *śruti* as a proof of truth. When I recently stated this technically undeniable situation to an Indian woman physician, she replied heatedly that she would be ashamed to call herself a Hindu just because of belief in the Veda. All good people are Hindus, she said, even if they do not believe in the Veda. This, of course, is a crass instance of that inane eclecticism which is part of modern Hinduism.

pounded the identity of Vedāntic, Communist, and *Bhagavadgītā* teaching. He was expelled from the mission and a more conservative monk has now been running the center for many years. Yet the attitude is not at all new in India, and it finds outlets in organizations less highly institutionalized than the Ramakrishna Mission.

But it is only the most sophisticated and de-ethnocentrized who know that all these models are imports from Europe, with no indigenous element in them. The idea that Hinduism, Buddhism, or Jainism teaches the creation of a better society is wholly wrong and quite jejune in terms of its motivation. The *Tripitaka* and the other Buddhist texts never speak in terms of political, international, or even intersocietal peace; they are solely concerned with the individual "psycho-experimental" processes that lead toward emancipation and that entail among other things emancipation from society. Society is not reformable; the wise man is the one who withdraws from it through meditation culminating in the core teachings of Buddhism and Hinduism. There are no two ways of interpreting the consummatory end of these two traditions. The ideal Hindu was and remains the one who succeeds in removing himself from familial and social commitments. Hindu political eclecticism wants to preserve the tradition by claiming that it has been modern all along, that it always taught people to be active in society. But since this is patently false, the modern Hindu cathects those statements about Hinduism which support the stipulated modernity; and this is precisely the kind of good the Hindu Renaissance, beginning with Vivekānanda, has been supplying. Though sociocentric Hinduism was never envisaged by its founders nor supported by its later proponents, the processes by which these teachings become sociocentric are all-important for our study.

4. The fourth aspect of modernized Hindu doctrine follows as a natural sequel of the third. It is the notion of the dignity of physical labor. This is completely new to India, a Western import. The allusions to manual jobs appearing in various *smrti*, though never in the *śruti*, are not reflections of an ancient or medieval re-

spect for physical labor, but rather exemplifications of obedience to some dharma, the rule wherein a person is born. The humble craftsman who does his job well and whom those texts eulogize for it, is not praised for seeing dignity in his work, but for accepting it as a punitive condition aiding his own spiritual advancement. No wonder that the governmental agencies have been singularly unsuccessful in impressing the concept of dignity of manual work on the peoples of South Asia. Defilement and ritualistic purity are so much a part of the traditional ideology that mere decree, however pragmatically conceived, cannot change the basic value orientation. Anyone who has learned to read and write, wants to read and write; he does not want to revert to manual occupations. This may be regrettable and it is certainly not conducive to the social and economic growth of India, but it is an anthropological fact. It is not the job of the social scientist qua social scientist to predict and laud possible changes in basic attitudes if they happen to be disfunctional.

5. The final point, no doubt the most sensitive and the most frustrating to the would-be sympathizer of the Renaissance, concerns the radical decline of aesthetic perception in modern India. It is hard to believe that a culture whose specialists have created marvelous and truly exciting works of art over fifteen centuries should have lost the traditional acumen in the arts and in their appreciation. This loss, however, has become an obtrusive fact. Not only the local cicerone but also the professor of economics at the University of Delhi, when asked to recommend sites of interest to the visitor, will mention the Qutb Minar, the Red Fort, and the Birla Temple. The latter is a dreadful structure created under the auspices of the oldest of the Birlas, one of the three or four top entrepreneurial Marwari families. Listing it along with the Qutb Minar and the Red Fort is very much like lumping together Saint Peter's, the Acropolis, and Disneyland.

A common sight in India today is the display of polychromes depicting gods and goddesses of the Hindu pantheon, saints, seers, politicians, film actresses, and other unlikely figures, all portrayed in a multicolored medium of gross realism inspired by certain Indian disciples of some minor and bad Victorian painters. These oleographs, ranging from postcard to poster in size, cover the walls of government offices, teashops, and private homes in urban areas; they have even appeared in temples. Indian business calendars using this sort of art work have wide currency in areas of the world where there is even the smallest settlement of Indian expatriates. These veritable monstrosities never seem to elicit critical remarks from an Indian audience. Professor Ainslie T. Embree of Columbia University, whose large collection of oleographs should some day provide material for a seminar on modern Indian art, posted several of them in his office and noted the reaction of Indian students and Indian fellow scholars. Political science graduates, sciologists, historians, and others passed by and not one seemed to object to what an art critic unconversant with the Indian situation today would consider a blend of late nineteenth-century seafarer art and exotic soap-opera scenario. The reactions of the viewers were positive and favorable: "Oh, you have our great people here," "Oh, it makes me homesick, it reminds me of pictures at home," "These pictures of the gods, just like in India." Indeed they were. If the inferiority of this kind of art is pointed out to any modern Indian, he changes the subject or remonstrates. The naïve idea pervasively present is that an artifact representing good and noble things could not be in itself bad. The distinction between good art and important content is simply not known to the modern urban Indian.

But it is also true that at the same time the traditional arts are being continued, with little sponsorship, by the *kalākāras* and by other traditional, although obscure, artisans all over the land. New, highly sophisticated painting is emerging in various schools, its practitioners followers of a group of academicians who have been under direct or indirect Western tutelage of a very high order.

Cutting through all these five points, a strange phenomenon pervades the subcontinent in its process of modernization. A somewhat facetious term for this phenomenon might be the "pizza effect." The pizza originated in southern Italy as a humble staple, a bread dish without any of the accouterments which we now associate with the Italo-American pizza. But when the *mafiosi* and other Sicilians and Calabrians brought it to the United States, it became, as it were, affluent in the proportion the settlers became affluent. Since about 1920 this modified pizza has been making its victorious reentry into Italy. At many places, north and south, pizza has become much the same dish as the one available in the United States. Something parallel to this has happened in South Asia. Cultural things formerly looked upon as archaic, "superstitious," and not conducive to the modern spirit, began to be sought out, their importance being positively reassessed on the merit of having been appreciated abroad. Satyajit Ray's Bengali film trilogy, to take an example, was originally a flop in Bengal and elsewhere in India. The average Indian movie-goer preferred to see chintzy stories of papier-mâché romance or of mythological royalty and divinity, while the more enlightened favored *sāmājik,* "social" stories with a message. Neither cared to see chunks out of Indian village life, which is poor and uninteresting. But when *Pather Panchāli, Aparājita,* and *The World of Apu* received awards at the Venice film festivals and high acclaim in Europe and America, things changed. In the past five years modern sophisticated movie-goers in India have come to praise these productions. The pizza effect benefited not only Satyajit Ray but, to a greater degree, the masters of Indian instrumental music such as Ravi Shankar, Alī Akbar Khan, Bismillah Khan, and Subbulaxmi.

This process, however, began much earlier than the twentieth or even the nineteenth century, although in recent times the reestablishment of Indic studies, of Sanskrit, and of concern for Indian religion and literature has assumed increasing importance. The eulogization of Max Müller as *moksamūla bhatta* ("root of salvation") and of his disciple Paul Deussen as *pāla devasena* ("protector of a divine army") by the pun-loving Brahmins reflected a renewed interest not only in the West but in India as well. The tête-à-tête between Swami Vivekānanda and Deussen, along with the dialogue of lesser Indian spiritual luminaries with various Western savants, kindled a new concern for Indian studies, which had been regarded as unproductive and irksome by the two generations of Indians who had come to regard English as the criterion of modernity. But long before Max Müller and Deussen the lore of India had aroused amazement and enthusiasm in the West. The first English translation of the *Bhagavadgītā* was published by Charles Wilkins in 1785, with a preface written by no less a person than Warren Hastings. The fact that the *Bhagavadgītā* has assumed an ideological importance far beyond its traditional place may be due to a concatenation of literary and historical events commencing with Wilkins' translation. But on the basis of the pizza effect it can perhaps be predicted that there will be a reevaluation of Indian sculpture and painting as well. As the West begins to buy *bharata nātyam,* Ravi Shankar, *sitars,* incense, saris, and even Natarajas in bronze, India may well forswear its polychrome *kitsch* and turn to its own tradition, aesthetically refined even though highly codified in its eidetic artifacts.

Yet another major issue lies in the state of Hindu culture and society taken in a much wider and anthropological sense. What modern Hindus learn from their parents, peers, and religious practitioners of many kinds, is something very different from the actual manner in which Indian society is being modernized. Again, the Indian villager is not primarily touched by these changes because he does not "modernize" and is marginal to the processes of ideological modernization which are located in cities. Whatever he experiences is channeled to him through the urban agents of the Indian Renaissance emanating from the city. Whenever a modern Indian makes the pronouncement that "caste has been abolished," he seeks to let the matter rest there, accepting the dictum quite uncritically. But if probed as to what he actually has in mind, it appears that he may be conceptualizing two or three very different themes.

He knows that observation of the rules of untouchability has been declared a punishable offense by federal legislation. But he confuses the formal abolition of untouchability with the abolition of the caste system, viewing untouchability as the *pars pro toto.* If a Harijan ("man of God, people of God") — the euphemism Gandhi created and institutionalized in summary reference to all people of the scheduled castes and tribes — insists on being served coffee and *dosa* at a Brahmin Coffee Club in Mysore and the shopkeeper refuses to serve him, the untouchable can file suit and the errant shopkeeper will go to jail. This does not mean that caste has been abolished, any more than that discrimination has been abolished by the passage of desegregation ordinances in contemporary America. More importantly, caste cannot be abolished by decree, since it *is* the social structure of South Asia. Hindus, Muslims, Christians, and Jains, all live within the system. It is not a system of value orientations as Indian moderns would have it, but one that rests primarily on the social fact of endogamy.

The modern Indian who claims that caste has been abolished, however, does not understand this, although when pressed by an expert whom he recognizes as such, he will attempt a statement of intermediary compromise: "Yes, this is true, but the system is breaking down or is about to break down. . . . We marry whomever we please. My friend married a girl outside his caste," and so on. It often seems to the observer that an enormous number of people must share the same friends, for marriage across caste lines is statistically insignificant, about .05 percent for the subcontinent. Except for some college students and others exposed to Western ways — roughly a thousand Indian males have married non-Indian women each year during the past decade — no one ever thinks of the possibility or even the desirability of marrying out. The minimal criterion of caste in South Asia is endogamy, and it seems to be as strong as ever.

Paradoxically, the perpetuation of the caste system aids the democratic process, because votes are obtained by appealing to the candidate's castemates rather than to any other sector of his constituency. The modern Indian, when reminded of this situation, tends to become annoyed, feeling that this is hardly the way to translate social modernization from a Western model.

Modern analytic philosophy provides tools of cultural analysis. The ordinary language approach, as formulated by Austin (1961, 1962), seems particularly suitable for analysis of the Hinduism of the Great Tradition. Such controlled analysis provides an instrument of cognitive assessment superior to the conservative forms of philosophical interpretation espoused with little result by virtually all Indian teachers of philosophy. Anthropologists, it is true, have not yet made up their minds about the sort of linguistic tool to be employed, or the philosophical system they should ally themselves to, when reporting phenomena of the Great Tradition. When the modern Indian says "caste has been abolished," what he really means to say is "caste ought to be abolished." In other words he makes an "is" statement when he should be making an "ought" statement, or, more precisely, he fails to make a situationally objective counterfactual conditional statement.

D. G. Mandelbaum believes that the modern informant does indeed make correct statements even though they are partially marred by his incomplete knowledge of the social situation which he shares, hence does not (usually) analyze.* But there can be disagreement with Mandelbaum on this count. Most vocal Indians are quite aware of the caste situation and the various strictures systematically enjoined in the endogamous setting of all South Asian societies. Whatever his degree of objective knowledge about the situation, the modern Indian tends to make such statements not only to Westerners, who are unaware of these complex matters, but also to other Indians, to Pakistanis, or to Ceylonese. He may or may not mean to say that discrimination on the basis of caste should go, but this has little if anything to do with his understanding of the system. All this is borne out by the fact that high caste Hindus, when speaking about their own ranking and the exalted historical or current status within neighboring groups, are eager to reiterate and to eulogize their own caste. On other occasions they may deride or deny the caste system per se by making such statements as the ones quoted earlier. Other Hindus of low caste status do not recount the glory of their ancestry. Among lower castes in India there is also a pervasive "upcasteing," a phenomenon studied

* Remarks delivered at the 1966 and 1967 annual meetings of the American Anthropological Association held at Pittsburgh and Washington, D.C., respectively.

in great detail by such observers as Cohn (1959) and Marriott (1952).

Perhaps the best way to challenge the misleading statement that caste is dead is to ask the speaker to make the same affirmation in his Indian vernacular. As has been suggested, it is impossible to do this; and many people will squirm at the suggestion, feeling it to be probably unfair and certainly improper. The closest approximation they can make in the vernacular is the one suggested earlier, i.e., "discrimination on the basis of caste has been abolished (redeemed, forgotten)." The neologism, probably introduced by Gandhi, is *jātibhed*, which in its classical connotation meant something like the "differential qualifications to carry out rituals, on the basis of caste." The neologized term is useful in all Gandhian forensic, and Congress speakers have no trouble employing it to disabuse their audience of these disfunctional, odious distinctions. Clearly, "caste" and "discrimination on the basis of caste" are two different things, and the succinctness of the Sanskrit composite may have contributed to the ease with which modern Indians try to dissimulate the situation. Any literal translation of "caste has been abolished (weakened, remedied)" would mean "the social structure has been abolished (weakened, remedied)," and is thus patent nonsense.

Another apologetic corollary is the confusion of *jāti* and *varna*, or the idea held by Sanskritized Indians that "caste" translates *varna*. Those who hold this view regard *jāti* either as an ancient degeneration of *varna* or as something quite different and not at all at issue. The lexeme *varna* goes back to Vedic literature; ivory-tower orientalists of the last century and the present probably believe that the Vedic prescription, which was a purely theoretical, literary, or ideally utopian device, did apply at one time and ought to apply now. The classical *varna*-formulation serves as an intellectualized non-factual "description" of a set of social postulates, which may or may not have been replicated by social fact at some time. To be a Brahmin by *varna* always raises the question "what Brahmin?" with the social scientist, as well as with Indians not ex-

posed to modernity. Again the Indian jingoist's view of things con-
verges with that of the scripture-oriented orientalist.

There are well over two hundred Brahmin castes in India, and if
we apply the minimum criterion of endogamy to signify "caste,"
then the term "Brahmin" is nonfunctional. Sārasvat Brahmins
from Mangalore marry Smārta Brahmins from Bangalore no more
than any Brahmin marries any *vaiśya* of the classical scheme. Nor
do the *pañca-drāvida* ("five southern group Brahmins") regard
the *pañca-gauda* ("five northern group Brahmins") as their
equals. They would not eat food cooked by them and there would
be no commensal interchange. In these sociologically central matters, very little has changed even among those people whose ideology and religious world view has turned modern and eclectic. The
fourfold *varna* system, when extrapolated as putative social fact,
lends itself admirably to the modern Gandhian and official Indian
notion that a man's caste is his skill, not his birth. For this, there is
absolutely no support in the *śruti*; the *smrti* vacillates and its am-
bivalence is harnessed to establish and confirm the official "secular" teaching that a man is what he can do, and not what he hap-
pens to be by birth.

A further paradigmatic statement is "we are not interested in
religion." What does this mean? A young Hindu leaves India,
studies at an occidental university overseas, and never talks about
Hinduism, believing more often than not that talking about religion will make foreigners laugh at him as old-fashioned. He may
also genuinely believe that he is not interested. When he returns to
settle in India, after abandoning his latent hope that he might
make a career abroad, he very often begins to catch up with ideas
which touched him only marginally before he left India. Of course,
it is too late and too difficult to learn to read Sanskrit or seek out
primary sources, but he will read Vivekānanda and other Renaissance authors. In spite of his Western sojourn, he will not object to
the polychrome pantheon on the walls of his home.

Hindu moderns, particularly those with an inherited identification with such new sects as the Arya Samāj and the Ramakrishna
Vivekānanda movement, and with such leaders as Sāī Bābā, Rad-

hasoami, Aurobindo, or Śivānanda, would call traditional practices "superstitions." But as elsewhere in the literate world "superstition" means any religious practice or belief system which the person who uses the term dislikes or has disavowed. There seems to be no other adequate definition of "superstition." But again the strange fact is that "superstition" cannot be rendered in an Indian speech form with adequate lexical or semantic equivalence. In Panjabi and Hindi-Urdu speaking areas, the term *andhā-viśvās* is commonly used to mean "superstition" by speakers of English and a northern vernacular. However, *andhā-viśvās* means "blind faith." This compound is a neologism created by the Hindu Renaissance, a coinage possibly first used by Dayānanda, who did not know English, but who must have intended "blind faith" as a criticism of all other forms of Hinduism and of the non-Indian religions: Christianity, Vedānta, all the *sanātana* or orthodox forms, and particularly the use of idols. The medieval Hindi connotation of *andhā-viśvās* seems to have been "gullibility" or "credulousness" and referred not to a sect or denomination but to individuals or types of persons within any belief system.

There is a parallel in Islam, where traditional, *'ulamā*-controlled votaries reject virtually everything that South Asian Islam has contributed to the Arab original. The worship of *pīrs, walīs,* other saints, and tombs, and pilgrimages to places other than Mecca have continuously drawn censure and wrath from the doctors of the *'ilm* but without avail. Muslim orthodoxy refers to all these observances as *waham* ("superstition"), to the extent that almost all the typically South Asian Muslim religious activities that have been added on to the Arab original are referred to as "superstitions" by spokesmen for the *'ulamā.*

In India any talk about modernization contains an implicit or explicit reference to technology in the Western sense. The term "scientific" as currently used by South Asians seems to translate as "technologically informed," rather than as "scientific" in the Anglo-American lexical sense. Whenever the occasion arises, this technological know-how is somehow transposed into ancient India.

This has become so much part of the general parlance of modern India that the ascription of major technological inventions and discoveries to the Indians of antiquity is an inalienable part of the nationalistic idea complex. Three examples should suffice: Sītā and the airplane, Rāma and the atom-bomb, and Arjuna and Argentina.

The airplane is claimed as a Western invention: not so, says the Hindu, for what was the *vimāna* or *puspakāyana* ("vehicle" or "flower chariot") that flew the reunited couple and retinue back to Ayodhya from Lanka, family-fare? Of course, it was the ancestral airplane! One cannot fly unless one has an airplane; what a superstitious idea to think that some sort of magical contraption was involved; on the contrary, that was the first airplane. Then somehow the West got wind of it and built the modern plane on ancient Indian recipes.

During the final battle of the Kauravas and the Pāndavas in the great Epic, several weapons were thrown and exploded, and their exact description ("like 10,000 suns bursting forth at the same time," "like a cloud of rays," etc.) reveals that the *Varunāstra* ("weapon of Varuna"), the *Brahmāstra* ("weapon of Brahma"), and the other divine -*astras* were atomic bombs. The frequent suggestion that Indians should be glad that it was not their ancestors who created the instrument for total destruction, is not understood by any but the most sophisticated — and I have heard at least three senior Gandhiites take objection to this sort of countersuggestion as "supersophisticated."

My third example concerns a worthy *subedar** of the Indian national army who, during Guru Nānak's birthday celebrations, told an audience of Sikh soldiers that the scriptures tell that Arjuna went to Patala, "the opposite part of the world." "For this reason," the *subedar* continued, "that country is called *Argentina*, for *Arjuna* visited it." Rarely is an Indian audience, even a modern one, amused by this anecdote.

---

* Before independence a *subedar* was an officer commissioned by the viceroy, as distinguished from the regular officers with royal commissions. The *jamedar* and the *subedar* (old Moghul military ranks by nomenclature) are now called junior commissioned officers.

The folklore etiology for the technology complex is even more bizarre: most if not all pandits in India believe that the Germans somehow made away with the Veda and transplanted it to Germany, creating their arms, planes, and other scientific equipment out of Vedic instructions. Just how and when this is supposed to have happened is by no means clear to anyone — nor, of course, is it important. There is also a pervasive notion that the German language is "closest" to Sanskrit, and any linguistic suggestion to the contrary — that, for example, all European languages with the exception of Hungarian, Finnish, and Basque are related to Sanskrit, or that the Slavonic languages are the closest — is met with unbelief and indifference. But the statement that German could not be closer to Sanskrit than English, for simple linguistic reasons, is rejected with anger and with a charge of imperialism. It would no doubt be interesting to trace the beginnings of this Teutonophilia: I have tried it elsewhere (1965), but the simple fact is that Max Müller and Paul Deussen had their admiring audience in India. The publication of the *Sacred Books of the East* in English must have been presaged, so the pandits will argue, by an edition of the Vedic texts in Europe.

The *śruti*, of course, was never written down until Western scholars undertook the work; the Vedic word was too sacred to be committed to writing — all other literature including the *smrti* was, but *śruti* would have been polluted by such an act. The hundreds of Brahmin *gotras* (agnatic lineages of seers and their male descent groups) preserved the memorized text, one *śākhā* or "branch" per *gotra,* and passed it on orally. When a *gotra* died out, its specific *śākhā* of the Vedic text vanished with it. Hence the universal Hindu notion that only a very small part of the Vedic hymns has been preserved. Crucial parts of the scripture, the Hindu believes, were taken out of India, probably by the Germans, and one must not ask when, why, and how. The logistics of this cloak-and-dagger venture do not seem to worry any pandit or any modern Hindu — it is the assumed fact that counts.

It has been said that India has never produced historians and that it lacks a sense of history. This is a somewhat glib statement, yet there is no doubt that the cyclical world view of indigenous Indian cosmology and the speculative systems presupposing such a view have been impediments to the development of a chronology-based historiography, unlike the situation in China or Europe. More positively, there is a strong tendency in modern India to de-chronologize or dehistoricize events that *must* have taken place. The process is of a dual sort. In the first place, the historic event, person, or item is not dated in the sense that dates are not asked, a point valid for hagiographic talk and writing. Thus Sikhs dislike hearing that Guru Nānak lived in the sixteenth century, and contemporary Sindhi and Gujarati Hindus do not like to say that Dada Chellaram died in 1946.*

Second, and more important, there is a totally unrealistic projection of Indian historical events and persons back into prehistorical or, rather, nonhistorical times. This poses a major problem for serious research. With the exception of Indians trained in occidental traditions of learning, scholars and students believe that the Veda, the Upanisads, the Epics, the Purānas, in fact, all scriptures and all the heroes mentioned in them, belong to an era many thousand years ago. Any suggestion that the *Rgveda,* for instance, was compiled between 1200 and 800 B.C., is met with genuine annoyance. Such notions are "European," they lack good will, they bespeak arrogance and colonialist pride. When ten university students at three large Indian universities and ten Hindu students at an American university were asked how old they thought the *Rāmāyana* was, eight of the students in India and four of the students in the United States said "many thousand years." Most of them were students of natural science or technology, but four were political scientists and one a geographer. None of these informants came anywhere close to the probable correct date. One of the men, at an Indian university, said the Epic was written a thousand years before the Buddha; since he happened to know the Buddha's date,

---

* Dada Chellaram was a Sindhi merchant and, like most Sindhis, a follower of Guru Nānak. His simple, pietistic teaching has attracted many followers among Sindhi, Cutchi, and Gujarati Hindus. Chellaram remained a "householder" all his life, i.e., he did not embrace monastic vows.

this notion still placed the *Rāmāyaṇa* about a thousand years earlier than its probable time of composition.

While actual dating is in itself considered meaningless in reference to items of Indian cultural origin, unless the date is very old, Indian apologists nevertheless take it as an insult. When the writer, as a young monk, was an editorial assistant at the Advaita Ashrama in the Himalayas, the publication center of the Ramakrishna Mission, he helped with the editing of a volume of Swami Vivekānanda's letters. In some of the letters Vivekānanda waxed eloquent about the wrong dating of Indian scriptures by Western scholars. His criticism no doubt included even his respected friend, Max Müller, whose dating of the Veda was highly accommodating and well beyond presently accepted antiquarian chronologies. To Vivekānanda, however, Müller was guilty of Western arrogance, for "in reality" the Veda was many thousands of years old.

One can perhaps hazard a guess as to the origin of these notions about Indian antiquity: the Veda is *apauruṣeya* ("not made by a human"), i.e., inspired by Divinity — hence the easy switch to its being eternal. Thus the outsider who persists in raising questions about inspiration is considered both arrogant and materialistic. At the Ashram, Swami Yogeshwarananda, then the president and a very learned man, treated the writer with scorn: "Are you a greater scholar than Tilak? Didn't he prove beyond any doubt that the home of the Vedas was in India and that the *rsis* first pronounced them over 25,000 years ago?" B. G. Tilak's *Arctic Home of the Vedas* (1955) has been much on the minds of both orthodox and Renaissance Hindus. However ludicrous his intentions and his premise, the sheer erudition that went into Tilak's *magnum opus* remains astounding. (Whether Tilak was convinced of his argument or whether he propounded it for purely ideological reasons is beside the point, though apparently he did believe what he wrote.) Nevertheless, the important point to be made here is that an antiquity of nonhistorical dimensions is part of modern Hindu thought; historical statements of a realistic sort are tagged as anti-patriotic.

Turning briefly to the political aspect of modernization, we may consider an illuminating anecdote involving the late Raghuvira, inventor of a "scientific Hindi" that his opponents call *Raghuvīrī*. A master of many trades in the Indological profession, Raghuvira happened to address a group of students and merchants at the Central Hindu College of Banaras Hindu University during the time of the Bandung Conference. He declared: "Those ignorant people in our government call Indonesia 'Hindeshia,' as though it were derived from 'Hind' (= India) + Asia. The fools! Don't they know that the correct meaning of Indonesia is *bhārata-dvīpa?*" Now it is quite true that Indo-nesia translates, morpheme for morpheme, into *Bhārata + dvīpa*, that is, "Indo + (Greek) *nesia.*" But the intention of Raghuvira's remonstrance was not linguistic; rather it was an instance of Indian cultural expansionism, the "Greater India" concept that is part of modernized, jingoistic Hinduism. *Bhārata + dvīpa* means "Indian islands," and the intention of the creators of the term "Indonesia" was very different indeed from that of latter-day Hindu nationalists. Divan Chaman Lall's *Hindu America* (1956) is a more famous and much grosser case in point. In the same vein dozens of Greater India pamphlets and books appear year by year, extending the cultural shores of India into wide regions of the Asian world.

There is a great deal of difference, it goes without saying, between a scholarly report on India's cultural diffusion into Southeast and Eastern Asia or into the Iranian West, and the ideologized version of history which chauvinistically treats India as a culture-giver to large chunks of the world. The latter has been a powerful theme in the dialectic of Hindu rightist groups, with its implication that a giver of culture should also be a ruler over the areas into which the culture spread. When the writer did fieldwork on the Indians in East Africa in 1964, he heard the senior leader of the small but well-organized Maharashtrian community at Dar es Salaam attempt to demonstrate that "Africa got all its culture from India in olden times." Why? "Because the Masai and the mChaga are tall and light-skinned." Tall and light-skinned means noble; and noble means of Indian origin.

Finally, the overriding characteristic of modernized Hinduism is puritanism, a topic which, for pedagogical reasons, has been kept to the end. In talking about modern Indian puritanism, I have in mind a slightly modified version of H. L. Mencken's definition: A puritan is a person constantly haunted by the nagging fear that somewhere in the world someone may be having fun, especially sexual fun. Modern Indian students who have been exposed to the West will maintain that there is no prejudice against sex in India. "Everybody enjoys" ("enjoy" being modern Indian English for "having sexual relations"). A graduate student of political science said, "All wrong, we don't mind at all. I don't mind Khajuraho." This of course is an advance; Indians generally were not aware of the temples at Khajuraho before the labors of Mulk Raj Anand brought them to their attention. When the late M. N. Roy asked Gandhi about his view of the erotic sculpture profusely visible on Indian shrines, Gandhiji retorted, "If I had the power, I would pull them all down." But these temples will not be torn down because Khajuraho and Konarak are tourist- and hence dollar-attractions. I was delighted to notice recently that the flagship *Jhānsī kī Rānī* of Air India had finely drawn *apsarases* and other pulchritudinous damsels from Khajuraho printed on the cabin wallpaper.

It is evident, in conclusion, that modernization in India follows a pattern which is uniquely Indian and not predictable by any sort of overall ethnological theorizing. The process of ideological modernization is not a direct one from traditional forms to a modernistic and westernized way of looking at the world and acting in it. From the tribal and low caste bottom of the ladder, the road to modernization goes through Hinduization and Sanskritization. The grass-roots Indian, in both village and town, does not turn modern at once. First he adopts those elements of thought and action which the elite abandoned when they became modern: the employment of Sanskritic ritual, the use of austere and puritanical types of social interaction such as abandoning a diet of meat and renouncing the remarriage of widows, and the assumption of a quasi-philosophical world view as contained in the Sanskritic literature. The elite are the people whose forbears underwent Sanskritization at an earlier time — it is a fait accompli and from this vantage point modernization can and does set in. The high caste Brahmin boy who is living in the West finds it easier to eat meat than does the member of a scheduled group who wants to be accepted by those people who regard meat-eating as defiling. Upcasteing one's group means giving up pleasant things, an activity for which Sanskritization is only another facetious name.

A tribal Santhal working at the Tatanagar steel mills or a person of a scheduled caste may ride a bicycle, drive a car, and listen to a transistor radio; he may wear short or long trousers. Patently, this is not what we were concerned with. When the steelworker goes back to his village, he may urge his kinsmen to act like good modern people and not like low castes, to stop eating meat, drinking liquor, and marrying widows. In his mind a knowledge of contemporary gadgets, and certain forms of hygiene is as much a part of being modern as is *not* acting the way his kinsmen used to act before the modern age. To him being modern means being like higher caste people; he does not like them, but he regards their ways as standards which must be emulated.

Unfortunately the political leaders of modern India have failed to realize this situation. B. R. Ambedkar, founder of the Indian constitution and culture hero of six million onetime outcaste Mahars whom he converted to Buddhism, would not have liked the term Sanskritization. But he himself was very much a product and an agent of this process. It is not the use of the Sanskrit language, but of the ways extolled by Sanskrit writing over two millennia which accounts for Sanskritic behavior. The Buddha said *na candasā* ("Don't use Sanskrit") to his disciples. Yet Pālī Buddhism is as Sanskritic as Vedānta. The modernization of people already Sanskritized implies direct change through reinterpreting, metaphorizing, and then gradually abandoning traditional ideologies and their incumbent rules.

REFERENCES

Anand, Mulk Raj
1957. *The Hindu View of Art.* New York: Asia Publishing House.

Austin, J. L.
  1961. *Philosophical Papers*, ed. J. O. Urmson and G. J. Warnock. Oxford: Clarendon Press.
  1962. *Sense and Sensibilia. Reconstructed from the Manuscript Notes by G. J. Warnock.* Oxford: Clarendon Press.
Bhagavan Dass
  1944. *The Essential Unity of Religions.* Adyar: Theosophical Publishing House
Bharati, Agehananda
  1965. "Hindu Scholars, Germany and the Third Reich." *Quest* (Bombay), 44: 74–78.
  1966. *The Tantric Tradition.* London: Rider.
  1968. "Great Tradition and Little Traditions: An anthropological approach to the study of Asian cultures." In *Anthropology and Adult Education*, ed. Th. Cummings. Boston: Center for Continuing Education.
Chaman Lall, Divan
  1956. *Hindu America.* 2 vols. Bombay and Delhi: Published by the author.
Cohn, Barnhard S.
  1959. "Changing Traditions of a Low Caste." In *Traditional India: Structure and Change*, ed. M. Singer, pp. 207–15. American Folklore Society Publications, Bibliographical and Special Series, vol. 10. Austin: University of Texas Press.
Gould, Harold C.
  1962. "Sanskritization and Westernization, Further Comments." *Economic Weekly* (Bombay), 14, no. 1: 48–51.
Gumperz, John J.
  1964. "Speech Variation and the Study of Indian Civilization." In *Language in Culture and Society*, ed. Dell H. Hymes, pp. 416–29. New York: Harper and Row.
Hymes, Dell H.
  1962. "The Ethnography of Speaking." In *Anthropology and Human Behavior*, ed. Th. Gladwin and William C. Sturtevant, pp. 13–53. Washington, D.C.: Anthropological Society of Washington.
Iyer, Raghavan, ed.
  1965. *The Glass Curtain between Asia and Europe: A Symposium.* London: Oxford University Press.
Marriott, McKim
  1952. "Social Structure and Change in a U. P. Village." *Economic Weekly* (Bombay), 4: 869–74.
Murti, T. R. V.
  1955. *The Central Philosophy of Buddhism: A Study of the Madhyamika System.* London: Allen and Unwin.
Opler, Morris E.
  1944. "Cultural and Organic Conceptions in Contemporary World History." *American Anthropologist*, 46: 448–59.
Potter, Karl R.
  1963. *Presuppositions of Indian Philosophies.* Englewood Cliffs, N.J.: Prentice-Hall.
Redfield, R., and Singer, M.
  1954. "The Cultural Role of Cities." *Economic Development and Cultural Change*, 3: 53–73. (University of Chicago Research Center in Economic Development and Cultural Change).

Riepe, Dale
  1961. *The Naturalistic Tradition in Indian Thought.* Seattle: University of Washington Press.
Roy, M. N.
  1966. *Materialism.* New ed. Calcutta: Renaissance Publishers.
Shils, Edward N.
  1961. *The Intellectual between Tradition and Modernity: The Indian Situation,* pp. 15–18. The Hague: Mouton.
Singer, Milton
  1959. "The Great Tradition in a Metropolitan Center: Madras." In *Traditional India: Structure and Change,* ed. M. Singer, pp. 141–82. American Folklore Society Publications, Bibliographical and Special Series, vol. 10. Austin: University of Texas Press.
  1966. "The Radha-Krishna *bhajanas* of Madras City." In *Krishna: Myths, Rites, and Attitudes,* ed. M. Singer, pp. 139–72. Honolulu: East West Center Press.
Srinivas, M. N.
  1952. *Religion and Society among the Coorgs in South India.* London: Oxford University Press.
Staal, J. F.
  1963. "Sanskrit and Sanskritization." *Journal of Asian Studies,* 22: 261–75.
Tilak, Bal Gangadhar
  1955. *The Orion: or Researches into the Antiquity of the Vedas* and *The Arctic Home of the Vedas.* New eds. Poona: Kesari Press.

} MANNING NASH {

Buddhist Revitalization in the Nation State · The Burmese Experience

Religion plays a peculiar and predominant role in the new nations of Southeast Asia. Fairly unanimous in their hopes for the development of their societies, these nations all strive to build modern states and economies, to provide widespread educational and welfare services, and to develop and enrich a cultural heritage with a distinctive symbolic cast. In this drive for modernization and national consolidation religion comes to be the locus of the attempt to build a national identity and cultural viability. Religious symbols condense the most pervasive of collective symbols, for religion is the belief system felt to be most indigenous and valuable — continuous with the pre-colonial past and something greater than the cultural possessions of the developed modern nations. In Southeast Asia, then, religion is inextricably intertwined with national identity, cultural creativity, and the craving for modernization in a distinctive Asian style.

The place of religion in the social system of a nation like Burma raises important theoretical and empirical issues for social science and for those who want to understand the cataclysmic and often convulsive changes involved in the modernization of Southeast Asia. The most interesting problem is: In what ways can religion abet or hinder the process of modernization? To break this question down into empirically relevant phrasing and scale is almost to advance a theory of religion and society. In the case of Burma — which I use as a model for mainland Southeast Asia because of my firsthand knowledge of its society and culture — the question may be slightly rephrased to ask: What is the role of Theravada Buddhism in the course of social change in Burma? For several reasons Burma is an especially suitable place to investigate the place of Buddhism in the process of modernization: Theravada is the religion of 80 percent of the Burmese population; under the leadership of former premier U Nu, Burma deliberately undertook to recapture the place it once held as world leader of Theravada Buddhism; in 1961 Buddhism was made the official state religion; and, finally, a secular military regime has recently come to power. There has thus occurred a set of historical shifts and involvements with religion that make Burma a virtual laboratory for the study of the role of religion in Southeast Asia.

The history of Buddhism in Burma is coterminous with the forging of the ethnic identity of the Burmese. Under Anawrahta in 1044 Theravada Buddhism became the official religion of king and court. The establishment of Buddhism as the legitimating symbol system for a monarch more than nine hundred years ago gave rise to features that still persist in Burmese Buddhism and in the political life of Burma. In the course of his struggle with a cult of "Ari" monks, apparently a decayed form of Mahayana Buddhism, Anawrahta codified a series of disparate animistic beings and forces into an official list of 37 *nats,* and varieties of this *nat* propitiation have persisted and grown. From the beginning, therefore, Theravada Buddhism in Burma contained Mahayana elements, incorporated animistic elements, and was associated with a charismatic royal charter. Buddhism was institutionally rooted in the king, the court, and the sangha (brotherhood of monks). All the monarchs of Burma aspired to the role of *Cakkavatin,* an idealized universal ruler who was at the least a defender of faith and on occasion even the Buddha-to-be, in accordance with the messianic vision in Buddhism (Mendelson, 1961). A group of monks maintained the sacred paraphernalia of royalty at the court, and the reigning monarch undertook a generalized support of the monkhood in exchange for the symbolic stamp by the sangha that aspirations to *Cakkavatin* were legitimate. Outside the sacred precincts of the walled palace, the monarch demonstrated his magico-religious claims by the rite of plowing and harvesting that ensured the fertility of the land and hence the prosperity of the peasantry. The chief concern of the monarch was to obtain Buddhist sanction for the royal, hereditary, and charismatic power, while the sangha for its part sought royal support and patronage.

Although in the time of the monarchy the court appointed a *thathanabaing* (head of the sangha) and various subsidiary *gainggyok,* or bishops, the essential structure of Buddhist organization in Burma was, and is, acephaleous and confined to a single *kyaung* (monastic building) or a small group of them under an eminent *sayadaw* or senior monk (Mendelson, 1960, 1961). The court-appointed officials mediated religious disputes via the ecclesiastical courts and intervened in instances of pongyi involvement with secular authority, but they did not form a true hierarchy of authority with levels of command and real power to sanction either positively or negatively. Then, as now, the social structure of the sangha was a loose federation of sects, with such authority as existed vested in the head of a single monastery, or at most of a cluster of monasteries.

The concern of the sangha is of course the teaching of the dhamma and the individual search for salvation. Over the course of Burmese history the sangha has been neither theologically innovative nor exceedingly active in missionary work among animists, pagans or non-Buddhists. Most of the sangha's effort has gone into teaching at the village level and into a study of the *Vinaya* rules for monastic discipline. The sects that now make up Burmese Buddhism are differentiated only by minor variations as to how the *Vinaya* rules are to be interpreted. Such rules make little difference to the laity.

In a real sense Buddhism is a religion of the virtuoso and centered on the monk. The functions of the laity are to provide material support for the sangha, to honor them, and to learn the dhamma from them. To the question of whether a householder can reach salvation, there is no fitting answer, for the layman who is seriously interested in salvation will become a monk. One social process that has kept the monks from further isolation from the laity is the permeability of the boundary between pongyi and layman. Until the British occupation, every male spent some months as a monk, and more recently it has been reported that at any given time about one of every ten males in Burma may be in a monastery (Tinker, 1959). As late as 1960–61, villagers around Saigaing and Mandalay frequently spent the traditional year and a half as a pongyi, and every male participated in the *shinbyu,* the monastic initiation. So all rural Burmese men, at least, have worn the saffron robe and tasted monastic life. Now, as in the past, the sangha is a loose church with little treasure, much honor, and a great capacity to sanction power but not to hold, lead, or capture it.

When the British finally toppled the Peacock throne in 1886, they did not directly undercut the status of Buddhism or the monkhood, but their policy of minimal interference with indigenous religion set in motion some processes which weakened Buddhism. The colonial administration failed to support Buddhism and did not appoint the usual court officers of sangha head and bishops. The denial of government-granted privileges to monks dimmed some of the symbolic sheen of the pongyi, and the establishment of secular, English-style education in the cities and some towns led to the downgrading of traditional education by the small, Western-oriented Burmese elite.

During the colonial period Buddhism still exercised an unshakable hold on the mind of the villager, but apparently some deterioration had set in among the monkhood. The novel *Tet Pongyi,* which appeared in 1935, excoriated the false and idle monk, and in the early 1960s the expression *Khit pongyi* was used in the Mandalay area for what U Nu called in the delta the "rogue in yellow robes." Buddhism continued for a time to be the hallmark of Burmese ethnicity and traditional national aspirations. The rebellion of Saya San in 1931 probably marked the end of religious, traditional nationalism as a social movement. From the charismatic, Buddhist magical discontent of Saya San, the nationalist torch went to the secular wing of the *Dobama* association, to the Thakins, and finally to the Anti-Fascist People's Freedom League coalition which under the leadership of Aung San secured independence in 1948.

In the years following independence there was a revival in Burmese Buddhism. Brohm (1957) has described part of this renewed interest and activity in the countryside. Other aspects of the revival were the convening of the Sixth World Council of Buddhism in 1954–56, and the building of the *Kaba Aye* peace pagoda. In the mid-1950s legions of monks from all the Theravada countries gathered in the great cave of *Maha Pasana Guha*, which could seat 10,000 persons, to recopy and issue an authorized version of the *Tripitaka,* the Pali canon. All these activities testify to the renewed interest in Buddhism, and indeed its magnitude was such as to merit the use of the term *revitalization movement* to describe it.

Why the spurt in Buddhism? What explanation can be given for the resurgence of religious activity in the 1950s and early 1960s? There seem to be three obvious reasons: first, the renewed association of Buddhism with Burmese nationalism and its cultivation as the unique, precious flowering of Burma's contribution to world culture; second, the renewal of government patronage to the sangha; and third, the special qualities of U Nu, who led and stimulated the revitalization movement. (It should be kept in mind, of course, that the revival movement rested on the belief system of the ordinary Burmese Buddhist and was fed by the symbol system at the village level, including all the elements of supernaturalism — the *nat* propitiation, astrology, alchemy, ghost beliefs, and demons and ogres [Spiro, 1967].)

More recently, since Burma has come under the secular leadership of General Ne Win, the revival has apparently lost its energy and momentum. Visible signs are the decay and neglect of the

Kaba Aye peace pagoda, the deemphasis on pongyi education and on the establishment of a Pali university, and the demise of the ban on the slaughtering of cattle. In retrospect it seems clear that the movement was relatively short-lived and depended on the charismatic personality of U Nu, who epitomized and extolled the belief system of the peasantry, upon which, at base, the revival rested. It seems clear too that political conditions deteriorated during the time of the revitalization, partly because Buddhism was made the state religion and partly because the government engaged in symbolic religious behavior while it neglected pressing economic and social tasks. One overwhelming social fact stands out: the Buddhist revival movement was not intrinsic to Buddhism itself, it tapped no sources of religious energy, it unleashed no wave of religious creativity. It was a creature of government, politics, and the personality of U Nu.

The fate of the Buddhist revival under U Nu suggests three related conclusions about the future role of religion in Burmese modernization. First, the believed-in and lived-in religion of the Burmese, as distinguished from the scripture in the *Tripitaka*, needs to be modernized and rationalized itself before it can, if ever, play a constructive role in Burmese development. Second, the modernization of religion in Burma, and probably throughout Southeast Asia, depends on an intellectual class that has confronted the conflicts of religion with the modern world, and not on the traditional, unreflective carriers of Buddhism. And third, religion needs to be institutionalized in such a manner that the mundane demands of the everyday world are ambiguously defined and related to sacred precept. A failure to institutionalize religion so that it stresses a salvation idiom rather than a clear code of precepts which govern mundane life, may be a drag on modernization.

Something of the scope and magnitude of the necessary modernization can best be understood by looking at the religion of the Burmese peasant, the monk, and the member of the political elite as their various belief and symbol systems actually operate in everyday life to motivate behavior, structure social action, and cognitively map reality for believers. This is a much different task than conning the Pali canon, drawing inferences about meanings of the scripture, imputing these meanings to actors, and then further extending the already tenuous chain of inference by assuming that these constructs are involved in everyday activity.

Most of what I know, in the contextual as against the textual sense of Theravada Buddhism in Burma, comes from villagers and village-based pongyis in the Mandalay-Saigaing region (Nash, 1963, 1965, 1966). From what I have read about the delta area, there are few major differences between these regions. There is often, it is true, a large gap between the villager and the traditional intellectual, but my contention that Buddhism must be modernized and rationalized refers to the bulk of the ordinary believers, to the knowledge, practice, symbols, and consequences of Theravada Buddhism for most of the Burmans in Burma. From the description and analysis that follow, it will be seen that many aspects of Buddhism are neutral, indifferent, or irrelevant to modernization, and that the tasks of rationalization are not great. The task of differentiating Buddhism from other systems of action apparently is similarly simple.

For the villager, there is no single word or idea corresponding to "religion" or "Buddhism." The manifest reason for devotion and ritual is summed up in the phrase *bokda batha.* This means that a man tries within the limits of his knowledge and his temperament to follow the path that the *Shin Hpaya* (Lord Buddha) taught. Although there are of course differences among individuals in knowledge of and devotion to the middle way to salvation, there is no public disbelief and, so far as I could learn, no scepticism. Everyone appears to subscribe to and honor convictions about the truth of the teaching of the Buddha, and to hold that the following of this teaching is the moral path, the aim of existence, and the highest, unquestionable good. This is not to say that the villager lives with a spiritual consciousness forever honed to a razor's edge or that the mundane, ordinary business of living does not consume most of the time, thought, and energy of the people. Nevertheless Buddhism, as the villagers understand it, is the master artifice for giving unity, coherence, and meaning to their personal lives and to the world in which they live.

The major ideas of village Buddhism rest on three pieces of knowledge: first, the ideas of *kan* and *kutho;* second, the folk version of the levels of existence and the corresponding bits of cosmology that are entailed; and finally the notion of the precepts and their observance. *Kan* is the bundle of ideas associated with destiny, fate, luck, and life chances. It is the whole sum of a person's past deeds, the moral balance of good and evil which goes on from existence to existence, now taking one corporeal form, now another. A person's *kan* is strengthened by adding *kutho* (merit) and weakened by accumulating *akutho* (demerit). Some people have a good moral balance and destiny, and others have a bad fate. *Kutho* and *kan* are not esoteric concepts to the Burmese, and they are invoked frequently to explain ill fortune.

Kan is the product of individual effort. Every person has built his own store and quality of *kan*. For the Burmese villager this particular life is the result of all previous life, of all previous good deeds and misdeeds. His present existence is an opportunity to add to or subtract from the individual moral nucleus, which will be reborn in some form in another existence. Everyone is aware of his responsibility for his own state and his future states, but this does not weigh heavily on a villager. First of all, this life is but one wedged in among countless past lives and unimaginable future ones. There is not much that can be done in a single existence to shift drastically the amount and quality of a person's *kan*. Furthermore, achieving *kutho* and building *kan* do not require special insight, knowledge, or religious experience, but rather straightforward activity and simple observance.

Finally *kan,* in this life, is not a steady single force operating in an undeviating direction. A person's fortune and luck fluctuate, and so does his *kan*. Whether the good or the evil aspects of one's *kan* are predominant only time and the actual course of events can disclose, and the villager believes that discovery of one's full and entire destiny is hardly worth losing sleep over. *Kan,* then, is inscrutable and invisible, but individuals can determine what sort and how much of it they have through the things they do, say, and think, while they are alive. Every human being already has a considerable amount and a favorable sort of *kan,* because being born in the human state means that the *kan* has been auspicious enough to avoid the nether worlds of the Buddhist hells, the animal states, and other lesser rebirth possibilities.

Villagers do not aspire to be reborn in the higher states of Buddhist possibility. The thought of the final stage when rebirth no longer takes place — *Neikban,* as the Burmese call Nibbana — is remote from villagers, and its mention as a possibility only elicits smiles. Nibbana is something that only the Buddha (three early incarnations, Gotama the fourth and historical Buddha, and the fifth one, Arimittiya, now in the Tusita heaven awaiting the right moment to become manifest) has achieved. It takes millons of years and a movement through all the possible states of existence to reach Nibbana. This possibility is beyond the active desire and expectation of any villager.

The understanding of how *kan* is built and *kutho* earned is the direct route for interpreting the belief and practice of village Buddhism. But some idea of the cosmological perspectives of a villager is needed to place the activities and belief in cultural context. Burmese Buddhist cosmology and cosmography are a version of an older Hindu set of beliefs. The peasant and the village monk do not refer to the written word for their version of the world. Their notions are the common ones that every adult can give, not the intricate pattern found in the higher learning of the *Abhidhamma.* Villagers know that there are three different worlds of existence. These *lokas* or worlds each have a characteristic kind of life. The upper *loka* has twenty levels of *byama* (Burmese for Brahma: gods), divinities who can never be reborn into the world of men. Their moral attainments in earlier existences entitle them to varied sorts of enjoyment: eating sumptuously, appropriating young maidens who grow on trees for their sexual gratification, and generally indulging sensual appetites. They are not concerned with the mundane world and are beyond entreaty or appeal. After eons some of them may move to the level beyond, above, and without the world, that is, the encompassing and embracing all of Nib-bana.

Below the twenty grades of *byama* there are six levels of *nats*. These are the Buddha *nats,* so called to distinguish them from the other *nat* spirits which play an important part in the lives of villagers. Buddha *nats* can be reborn as men or they may ascend to levels above, but while they are *nats* they have no contact with the world of men. Below these twenty-six levels of the *deva loka* or spirit world is the level of men, the world in which villagers physically exist. This is the level of existence, of birth and rebirth, the plane on which *kuth* and *akutho* are accumulated, where *kan* is formed. And lastly there is the *loka* of the hells, populated by suffering animals, monsters, and people in flames, where there are many sorts of punishments and afflictions to bear. This world is the place of expiation for lives badly led, and it remains a possibility for those now in the *loka* of people. The hierarchy of existence is geared to moral attainment, to the state of *kan.*

In this sense, *kan* is closer to the English word "consciousness" than it is to the idea of destiny. Some sort of consciousness goes from material embodiment to material embodiment. Villagers claim, and the local monks support them in this belief, that no one remembers his past lives and that there is no individual continuity in the flux of birth and death. Yet in Upper Burma tales about people who do recall their former lives are received with belief, not incredulity. There is, however, a penumbra of ambiguity surrounding the idea of awareness. On the manifest level villagers speak of *anatta,* the idea of no self, in the sense of no individual continuity with a time-spanning awareness. But in many acts and statements villagers behave as though they believe that some essence of awareness with temporal durability and a history goes on from existence to existence. The pure notion of no self, a difficult philosophical notion at best, is reworked by peasant experience into an idea containing possibilities of self and self-continuty. But the matter is not pressing and debate on it cannot be long sustained.

Each person is believed to comprehend just so much of the profound words of the Buddha as his previous experience and moral state permit. If individuals differ on meaning or interpretation, this does not give rise to theological debate but merely indicates that people have different capabilities for absorbing and comprehending the teaching. Village Buddhism is thus the sort of religion where factions, theological debate, and questions of orthodoxy or heterodoxy cannot and do not arise. It is not so much that each man is his own temple, although this is surely true, but rather that each mind, each *kan* or temperament, is a particular sort of instrument for the refraction of the truths the Buddha enunciated. And because the individual prisms diffuse different parts of the spectrum, no one believes that there are many different truths and teachings, only that there are necessarily many sorts and grades of approximation to the truth.

The hierarchy of states of existence governed by *kan* is set into a physical geography which has as its ultimate source the same Hindu background as the levels of beings. On earth (*pahtawi*) are the living things, plants, animals, men, all of the metal-bearing rocks and soil and the hills. On this flat earth are four continents. Above the earth rises a high mountain, *Myinmodaung*, and above that are the levels of existence higher than the human. The four continents spreading out from the base of Myinmodaung are the East, West, North and South continents. They are also called in speech right (South), left (North), front (East), back (West) continents. Associated with the front and right continents is *mingala* (auspiciousness) and so East and North are preferred directions for ritual, sleeping, and other important activities, while West and South, being inauspicious, are associated with death, as well as with cooking and other lesser activities. Each continent has its particular people, its rivers, and its streams. This cosmology is the setting for understanding much of what goes on in Buddhism, in *nat* worship, in medicine, in divinatory and predictive systems, in choosing directions for travel, and in distingushing auspicious from inauspicious occasions.

Capping the cosmology is an apocalyptic vision. The apocalypse is the end of the present world and the coming of the fifth Buddha to begin the next world. The next Buddha, Arimittiya, is now in one of the levels of *nat* (upper) country. The present Buddha, Gotama, founded an era of five thousand years' duration that is now just about half over. At its end seven suns will appear in the sky and every living thing will, along with the world, disappear. This vision of the cycle of the world and its ultimate end does not affect peasant behavior. It is much less like the Christian notion of the Second Coming, which at times has flared into an active hypothesis, than it is like the second law of thermodynamics, where the tendency to entropy makes no difference to plans, hopes, or activities. Some men, however, have cults built around them and they are reputed to be nearing Buddhahood. These *weikzas* attract followers from the cities and the villages of Upper Burma, and their messianic movements have a potential for political and social change. Up to the present time, however, they have remained semi-subterranean personalized cults without impact on Buddhism or on the majority of its followers.

The village Buddhist world view can be summed up in the continually heard refrain: *aneiksa, dokhka, anatta* — change, suffering, no self. This is a shorthand for the truth of the middle way; it sums up what the Buddha discovered at his moment of enlightenment beneath the Bo tree. The middle way (*bokda batha*, the true wisdom) is a means of ultimately breaking out of the cycle of change and pain and false attachment to an ego. It is proximately the chief guide to morality and the bench mark against which the building of *kan*, the unending accumulation of *kutho* and *akutho*, go on. The main teaching is embodied in the *Mekgin Shitpa*, roughly translated as the Eight Virtues and more commonly called by non-Buddhists the Noble Eightfold Path. The noble truths are embodied in the *aneiksa, dokhka, anatta* formula.

The action aspect of the Eight Virtues lies in the five precepts. The precepts — not to kill, not to steal, not to engage in sexual misconduct, not to lie, and not to cloud the brain with intoxicants — constitute the minimal code that is not to be violated. Violation brings in its wake *akutho*, and breaking the first precept is the worst form of getting *akutho*. If a villager does not observe the precepts, he does not sin, for these are not divine commandments.

What he does do is move his moral balance in the wrong direction, making it more difficult for him to find the perfect peace. Observing the precepts builds good *kan* and also has the imputed effects of making one generous, without strong craving, respectful of elders, attentive to pongyis, and generally well regarded by one's neighbors. On special duty days *(ubonei)*, which are linked to phases of the moon and occur four or five times in a calendrical month, some people add three or five more precepts to be observed for a specified period.

The "Awgatha" or "wheel of life" devotional utterance which opens all gatherings of Buddhists, as well as some repetition of the *Mingala Thok*, some parts of the heart and diamond *suttas*, some of the Jataka tales, analogies and explanations from some of the Pali canon, and the omnipresent intonation of the "Triple Jewel" (I take refuge in the Buddha, I take refuge in the monkhood, I take refuge in the teaching) encapsulate the cosmology for the villager. They are the true collective symbols which enable him to encounter and to think about Buddhism.

The chief activities involved in being a Buddhist are those concerned with giving, with observing the annual ritual round, and with sustaining the monkhood. It is the act of freely-offered giving that positively adds to *kutho*, that makes the increments of morality into a heap of goodness, an engine of destiny that can move a person into a better plane of existence. Giving, meditation, devotion, and pilgrimages have the same kind of ultimate effect. By sacrificing something of the self, by concentrating on something other than the self, the bundle of sensation and desire that constitutes the self is purified, made less demanding. The villagers tend to think of *kutho* in amounts, in heaps, in quantities, but it is a negative sort of thing: the more *kutho*, the less the self is that sort of self having attachments to those things appealing to the craving for the fruits of the phenomenal world.

Giving constitutes the means, the positive volitional acts of building *kutho*, of refining the nature of the self. The act of freely giving is in a strict sense the Buddhist rite of sacrifice. Religious sacrifice is nothing other than offering one's self in exchange for religious fulfillment, for that sense of unity with whatever it is that makes the universe what it is. Sacrifice need not be total: one can give parts of the self or things the self is attached to, or even the dreams of the self, or intermediaries for the self. In this sense sacrifice is a graded system of merging identity with a cosmic consciousness. Both the temporal duration and amount of self that can be merged, of course, differ from world view to world view. In the end the successful Buddhist makes a complete and everlasting merger in *Neikban*. Giving is the lowest rung but an absolutely necessary one in this process of sacrificial merger with the universe. It is the activity supremely open to the ordinary Buddhist.

The effects of this symbol system are evident in daily political and social life. Buddhism is neutral about most occupational and vocational possibilities, a neutrality that has some consequences. There is no moral urging to do the world's work, but on the other hand there is no religious tradition that despises work or fixes a person to a small number of ways of earning his livelihood. In the temporal spacing of the life of villagers, there are elements favorable to a high commitment of human resources to economic activity. Villagers say that a man should apportion his allotted span in this fashion: From the age of 1 to 20 on learning and knowledge, from 20 to 40 on seeking fortune and wealth, from 40 to 60 on reducing working and enjoying leisure, and from 60 onward to thinking about salvation. This loose life plan keeps people in the labor force during their most vigorous and productive years.

Where Buddhism cuts directly into economic life is the costly business of facade, display, and monument building. On the basis of annual expenditure patterns, I computed that religious donations are about 14 percent of the annual outlay of a rich family, about 4 percent of a moderate family's outlay, and about 2 percent of a poor family's outlay. The wealthier a person becomes, the more, absolutely and relatively, he spends for religious ends. This orientation not only uses capital but grades the ends of activity so that merit-making — self-movement toward *Neikban* — is the highest unquestioned good.

Another double-edged effect of Theravada Buddhism is the extreme emphasis on the individual. Buddhism is an individuating system of belief; it places at the center of moral concern the fate and destiny of a single individual bundle of *kan*. This individualism has the effect of inhibiting the formation of groups above the domestic level of organization. Buddhism makes it difficult for villagers to participate in hierarchical, task-oriented, and authority-structured organizations. But this same individualism contributes to an equalitarian society. In Burma there are no fixed hereditary status divisions, no tight class systems, no places in the social structure to which even the humblest person may not aspire. There is the notion that outcomes are closely geared to individual effort. Even the idea of *kan* as the principal cause of what befalls a person is tempered by the accompanying ideas of *nyan* (wisdom or knowledge) and *wiriya* (work and industry).

Burmese life has the dual quality of appearing as a series of rather unconnected, immediate instances without much tie to the past and with little concern for the future, and at the same time of being filled with energetic beginnings of projects which fizzle out and leave nothing in their wake. This quality seems to stem from the Buddhist emphasis on long, vague time periods, the notion of one passing existence wedged in among countless others. This gives a time horizon that is not conducive to good planning and to effective execution. Without the constraint of meeting a standard at a given time, personal plans have an open-ended, unserious sort of vagueness about them. But on the other hand failure is not discouraging. Burmans bounce back quickly from defeat; they are never long sunk in apathy, and they have a generally cheerful, optimistic outlook on the world and their condition.

I have stressed the multiplex features of the effects of Buddhism on society and individuals. There is room for different emphases even in village Buddhism, and what is stressed depends upon the local monkhood and upon the political leaders of society. I forego too a description of the whole realm of *nat* worship, alchemy, astrology, ghosts and ogres — an integral part of Burmese religion. But these elements of supernaturalism are necessary to the functioning of Theravada Buddhism in Burma. They handle the immediate daily crises in a religious idiom, while Buddhism is the idiom of salvation. Burmese animism and predictive and divinatory systems are the technology of the sacred, and as such they are open to empirical inspection when in competition with the technology of science. That they have persisted and play such a large part in the villager's life is due to the small exposure the peasants have had to science, to modern education, and to a sophisticated segment of the monkhood. The ordinary pongyi usually shares the villager's animistic belief system as well as his Theravada Buddhism.

This symbolic set of Theravada and its accompanying animism provides a reserve for traditionalist political leaders to draw upon. The political successes of U Nu were in large part due to his ability to mobilize Buddhist sentiment, to display traditional piety, to embody the religious life, and to exemplify the virtues of the middle way. However, his kind of revitalization of Buddhism did nothing to make it more rational, more modern, more conducive to the urgent problems of national consolidation and economic recovery and growth. The florescence of Buddhism under U Nu stressed the most traditional, peasant aspects of Theravada, and even raised *nat* worship to national importance. Since the curtailment of the traditional Buddhist revival by the military government of General Ne Win, the task of harnessing some elements of Theravada to the problems of Burma has not been seriously essayed. Burmese intellectuals, in or out of the monkhood, have failed to come to grips with the problems of an ideology suitable to a modern, industrial, and ever-growing society. They have searched the doctrines of Marx for the key to an ideological breakthrough, but the many tracts attempting to show that Marxism is but the secular expression of Buddhism are singularly unimpressive and have little effect on the peasantry.

An ideology that will eventually help guide Burma through the transition to modernity must rise from the national experience along the route of social change. Traditional Buddhism and animism have already been displayed as poor ideological vehicles for this transformation. Marxism is also merely rhetoric in the Burmese context and not an efficient guide for policy. Living ideologies, either secular or religious, treat problems that arise from actual experience. They are the symbolic condensations of the meaning of experience and are a shorthand for coping with that experience. What Buddhism will become in a modernized Burma is, of course, problematic, but the symbolic repertory of Buddhism contains a strain adaptable to modernity. There is a basis for austerity and puritanism in Theravada, and it is possible to emphasize more proximate religious goals than Nibbana. And it is easy to envision the shrinking and decay of animism in the face of modern science.

The Theravada of Burma grew up in a society where structural change was minimal. Viable Theravada faces the task of becoming the ideological harbinger of massive and thoroughgoing social change. Either the small intellectual group in Burma will adapt Buddhism to this end, or else the future of Buddhism will become as problematic as it is in Japan. A final prognostication is that some form of aggressive nationalism, flavored by Buddhism and spiced with clichés from Marxism, will be fashioned as the ideological element in the drive to modernity. The brief spectacular revitalization of Theravada was, in my opinion, the last flare of traditional religion paving the way for a more pragmatic, realistic, and energizing symbol system for a nation that has no option but to modernity.

REFERENCES

Brohm, John F.
    1957. "Burmese Religion and the Burmese Religious Revival." Ph.D. dissertation, Cornell University.
Mendelson, E. Michael
    1960. "Religion and Authority in Modern Burma." *World Today*, vol. 16, no. 3 (Royal Institute of International Affairs).
    1961. "A Messianic Buddhist Association in Upper Burma." *Bulletin* of the School of Oriental and African Studies, University of London, pp. 560-82.
Nash, Manning
    1963. "Burmese Buddhism in Everyday Life." *American Anthropologist*, 65: 285-95.
    1965. *The Golden Road to Modernity*. New York: Wiley.
    1966. *Anthropological Studies in Theravada Buddhism*. Yale University Southeast Asia Studies, Cultural Report Series, no. 13.

Smith, Donald Eugene
    1965. *Religion and Politics in Burma*. Princeton: Princeton University Press.
Spiro, Melford E.
    1967. *Burmese Supernaturalism*. Englewood Cliffs, N.J.: Prentice-Hall.
Tinker, Hugh
    1959. *The Union of Burma: A Study of the First Years of Independence*. 2nd
        ed. London: Oxford University Press.

⟩ AZIZ AHMAD ⟨

Islam and Democracy
in the Indo-Pakistan Subcontinent

Gladstonian liberalism made a certain impact upon India, including Muslim India, during the viceroyalty of Lord Ripon in the
early 1880s. This influence took the form of the election of representative bodies for municipalities and other minor divisions of
local government. It was in such an atmosphere of political liberalism that the Indian National Congress had its beginning in 1885
and that the reaction of subcontinent Muslims to Western democracy was first formulated. The position taken by the Muslim consensus in 1887 vis-à-vis the Congress indicated their apprehensions
about the application of democracy to India, where it was bound
to be composite with an overwhelming majority of Hindus.

To Sayyid Ahmad Khān (1817–98) and to the Muslim consensus which he led, democracy meant the predominance of Hindus over Muslims. In the 1880s, and indeed until the partition of
the subcontinent in 1947, Muslims were essentially backward, relative to the Hindus, in education, economic enterprise, and political
consciousness. Thus for Sayyid Ahmad Khān Muslim participation in Indian democracy implied a politically unprepared and

immature participation, which he feared would lead either to a Hindu economic and cultural stranglehold or to a struggle for power. To avoid either of these outcomes, he advocated continuation of the British presence in one form or other. This Aligarh loyalism, as it may be termed, lasted from 1887 to 1911. It reflected a purely political fear of democracy; there was no theoretically religious element involved in it. In fact, during this period the *'ulamā*, or at least the influential section of them centered at Deoband, were anti-British and therefore pro-Congress. Of these *'ulamā*, Rashīd Ahmad Gangohī went so far in his repudiation of Sayyid Ahmad Khān's modernist views as to denounce his political stand and recommend a tactical alliance with the Hindus, though with the proviso that if "an association with the Hindus would lead to the commission of an act contrary to the *sharī'a*, or if it might cause depredation or humiliation of the Muslims, or if it might even assist the progress of the Hindus then it is expressly forbidden." [1]

These Muslim political attitudes toward the advent of composite Hindu-Muslim democratic development gradually changed with the passage of time. From 1908, on the eve of the Minto-Morley reforms, Muslim spokesmen came more and more to reconcile themselves to the inevitable growth of the democratic institutions for which the Congress was pressing. But they sought to protect Muslim political, cultural, and economic interests by demanding two political concessions within the democratic framework. One of these was for separate electoral bodies for Muslims, and the other was for weightage, or a larger percentage of Muslim representation in elected councils and assemblies than the actual proportion of the Muslim population would otherwise allow. On the basis of these safeguards the Muslim political parties, first the Muslim League and then the Khilāfat Conference, sought alliances with the Congress between 1911 and 1924, the years of Muslim disillusionment with British policies in India and with developments elsewhere in the Muslim world. The chief landmark of these alliances was the so-called Lucknow Pact agreed to by the Congress and the league in 1916. For some years after World War I Muslim polity assumed a revolutionary tone. This phase ceased with the abolition of the Sunnite caliphate in Turkey in 1924, an event which was accompanied on the subcontinent by the end of the Congress-Khilāfat alliance. The Muslim theological view during this period is best represented by Mahmūd al-Hasan of Deoband, who qualified *jihād* as nonviolent according to the teachings of Gandhi in British India, and who approved of Muslim participation in the Indian movement for political freedom. This, however, was conceptualized strictly in accordance with Muslim juristic precepts. Muslim participation was to avoid all action leading to chaos or excess and it was expected to support Hindu policies only so far as they were not harmful to Muslims. At the same time Mahmūd al-Hasan was apprenhensive of the possibility of economic exploitation of Muslims by Hindus.[2]

The years between 1924 and 1940 saw the political gulf between Hindus and Muslims widening. During this period Muslim political thinking, while still stressing safeguards within common democratic development, came to concentrate more and more on Muslim self-rule in the provinces and in the areas of Muslim majority in the subcontinent. This political separatism found its most explicit expression in the poet-philosopher Muhammad Iqbāl's presidential address to the Muslim League in 1930. Iqbāl's concept of Muslim politics was religio-political: "Islam does not bifurcate the unity of man into an irreconciliable duality of spirit and matter. In Islam God and the universe, spirit and matter, church and state are organic to each other." Within this conceptual framework Iqbāl developed his theory of Pakistan: "The principle of European democracy cannot be applied to India without recognizing the facts of communal groups . . . The Muslim demand for the creation of a Muslim India is, therefore, perfectly justified."[3] Iqbāl's concept of a Muslim state was, however, still that of a democratic state. His position is clarified in a letter written to Jinnāh in 1937: "For Islam the acceptance of social democracy in some suitable form and consistent with the legal principles of Islam is not a revolution but a return to the original purity of Islam."[4]

When the Round Table Conferences convened by the British

government in the early 1930s failed to arrive at a kind of blueprint for the future constitution of India, the joint committee on the Indian constitutional reform (1934) summed up the position of the future of composite democracy in the subcontinent in these words: "Parliamentary government, as it is understood in the United Kingdom, works by the interaction of four essential factors: the principle of majority rule, the willingness of the minority for the time being to accept the decisions of the majority; the existence of great political parties divided by broad issues of policy, rather than by sectional interests; and finally the existence of a mobile body of political opinion, owing no permanent allegiance to any party and therefore able, by its instinctive reaction against extravagant movements on one side or the other, to keep the vessel on an even keel. In India none of these factors can be said to exist today. There are no parties as we understand them, and there is no considerable body of political opinion which can be described as mobile. In their place we are confronted with the age-old antagonism of Hindu and Muhammedan . . . representative not only of two religions but of two civilizations."[5]

Muhammad 'Alī Jinnāh's "two-nation theory," based on similar arguments, denied the possibility or feasibility of composite democracy in India, but it affirmed the principle of democracy within the context of separatist Muslim nationalism, confined to the areas of Muslim majority in the subcontinent. According to Jinnāh, "Western democracy is based and inevitably brings about vertical rather than the horizontal divisions democracy envisages."[6]

The resolution of the Muslim League passed on March 26, 1940, at Lahore, popularly known as the "Pakistan Resolution," was the official Muslim demand for the Muslim state which came into existence in 1947. Meanwhile the Muslim League continued its struggle strictly within a democratic framework and there was no question that it envisaged Pakistan as anything except a modern democratic state.

But the transition from colonial democracy to political democracy in 1947 was sudden and demanding. The constituent assembly of Pakistan was obliged to function both as a constitution-making body and as a legislature. Soon after independence the government of Pakistan and its leadership faced a religious challenge. Most of the *'ulamā* in the subcontinent had been opposed to the creation of Pakistan, but the few who had supported the demand for it, with Shahbīr Ahmad 'Uthmānī at their head, gained considerable influence. They were joined by a number of other *'ulamā* who migrated from India. A fundamentalist movement—that of Abu'l A'lā Mawdūdī's *Jamā'at-i Islāmī*, with clear-cut political ambitions — was also transplanted to Pakistan. This small minority of theologians and fundamentalists had a certain degree of impact on some politicians and came to exercise some influence on the non-Westernized lower-middle classes with the demand that Pakistan should become an Islamic rather than a Muslim state (the former a religion-based system, the latter a nation in which Islam is the dominant religious faith).

The concept of the Islamic state in the minds of the theologians was of one which could be run according to the Hanafī law. For the fundamentalists, it was to be based on the externalist interpretation of the injunctions of the Qur'ān and the *Sunna*. In historical terms both the *'ulamā* and the fundamentalists regarded the state that existed under the orthodox caliphate as the ideal Islamic state. Thus they tried to impose upon the constitution-makers what they considered to be elements of democracy in that ideal in order to create in Pakistan a traditionalized Islamic state. This *Rāshidūn*-classicism is indeed an obscurantist throwback. G. E. von Grünebaum has defined it as the "classicism of return." Its object, he writes, is "in part at least, a decrease in cultural complexity . . . Such a movement characteristically overlooks the fact that the period of apostolic simplicity, which is chosen as authoritative and exemplary, was actually a period of experiential expansion."[7]

One must ask at the outset whether there are really any elements in early Islam which might serve as guidelines for the evolution of what may be termed Islamic democracy in Pakistan. In pre-Islamic Arabia the tribal leader or shaykh was not an absolute ruler. He was advised by a tribal council of elders or *majlis*. At the time of the advent of Muhammad, the various subtribes which constituted the Quraysh—those interrelated in the commercial community of Mecca—had a common council, the *malā*, drawn from the *majālis* (councils of elders) of the constituent tribes. The Meccan opposition to Muhammad thus had economic and political as well as religious causes. Meccans feared that the egalitarianism preached by Muhammad might affect their economic monopolies and that their oligarchical republican rule might break down under the authoritarian impact of the message and personality of Muhammad, who claimed to be the Messenger of God.

Muhammad's prophetic authoritarianism was lent force in political decisions, whenever they were not inspired by divine revelations, by the principle of consultation. This principle included the possibility of distinct differences of opinion among his most faithful adherents, some of whom, for example, criticized the Peace of Hudabiyya which he concluded with the Meccans in 628 as unfavorable to Muslims. As a result some of the Companions gave the Pledge of Good Pleasure (628), promising to abide by whatever decisions he might make in any matter. The pledge was blessed in the Qur'ān.[8] The principle of *shūra* or mutual consultation is recommended in the Qur'ān. One of the *sūras* (chapters), later given the name *Shūra* (Counsel), upholds the principle of mutual consultation among Muslims.[9] It is thus clear that some kind of ad hoc consultation took place in the light of the Qur'ānic injunctions under Muhammad and under his successors, the orthodox caliphs. But there is no basis for the theory advanced in India by Shiblī Nu'mānī during the last years of the nineteenth century and by Muslim modernists or apologists in other lands that 'Umar or any other orthodox caliph had a regular council or assembly or cabinets to advise him.

The actual historical position has been summed up with dramatic simplification by H. A. R. Gibb: "The occasion was the election of the third Caliph, in succession to 'Umar in 644, when (whether on the instructions of 'Umar or not) all the probable candidates of the succession assembled to debate the matter in *shūra* or Committee. Together with this instance, some modern writers have deduced from the references in the historical sources to 'Umar consulting with other Companions (read in the light of the injunction to consultation between the Believers found in the Qur'ān), the existence of something like a regular *shūra* during the Caliphate . . . But there is, in fact, nothing in the texts to justify the suggestion that 'Umar's consultation was more than informal or that there was at Medina any recognized consultative committee, still less a cabinet."[10]

All the same, even in the premodern period some theologians continued to hold the view that *shūra* was a desirable institution in the caliphate. In the subcontinent the fundamentalist Shāh Walī-Allāh (1703-62), writing long before any modern challenge exercised an influence on Indian Islam, argued that the Qur'ānic injunction on *shūra* refers specifically to 'Umar, "whose eminent quality was 'consultation.' No order was promulgated during his caliphate without consultation with the learned among the (Prophet's) Companions. During his caliphate consensus was reached on those matters which are considered most important by the Muslim community."[11]

In India British rule precluded the introduction of even the preliminaries of colonial democracy before 1883, but other Muslim countries felt the influence of Western democratic institutions earlier. In these countries the classical concept of *shūra* was equated, though in the beginning unapologetically, with modern Western consultative institutions. One of the earliest instances occurs in the Ottoman Empire when on the occasion of the enthronement of Mahmūd II in 1808 some notables convened an unprecedented meeting of a consultative body, the *Meclis-i Meṣveret*.[12] In Egypt Muhammad 'Alī named one of his consultative bodies *majlis al-mashwara* in 1829.[13] In Turkey the Gülhana Rescript of 1839 was partly based on a protocol prepared by a consultative council which was called *majlis-i shūra*.[14] In 1866 Khedive Ismā'īl of Egypt titled his consultative assembly *majlis shūra al-nuwwāb*.[15] In these early instances the use of the term *shūra* and its derivatives was not apologetic, but an effort to translate a modern concept into classical terms.

Probably the first apologetic equation of *shūra* with the institutions of parliamentary democracy appears in the writings of the Turkish poet and political thinker, Namik Kemal, who in the 1860s propagated the Western view that the "right of sovereignty belongs to all." He equated it with the classical concept of *shūra* by stressing that the binding thread of civilized society is the *sharīʿa*, "which is the political law serving to protect and govern members of society jointly and severally. Its interpretation is determined by the assent of the community but its basis is natural law. For us that natural law is the same divine justice as has been set by the Koran."[16] In the new, apologetic religio-political sense, Namik Kemal frequently used the term *meshveret*.

It is doubtful whether the views of Namik Kemal traveled to Islamic India until very recently. But in the 1880s Shaykh Muhammad 'Abduh held similar views with which Muslim Indian theologians were quite familiar. Shiblī Nuʿmānī, following the lead of Shāh Walī-Allāh, insisted in 1898 that Caliph 'Umar's government was run consistently on the theory and practice of *shūra,* which according to him was a consultative assembly consisting of permanent members.[17] Shiblī equates this early phase of Muslim orthodoxy with the cabinet of a modern parliamentary democracy, and in fact prefaces his work by contrasting democracy and autocracy. He goes on to argue that 'Umar's administration can be regarded as democratic, whereas those of the northern Arab kingdoms of the Lakhmids and the Ghassānids at the time of the Prophet were autocratic, as were also, of course, the Byzantine and the Sassanid empires. Shiblī concludes: "Without having any pattern or example before him, 'Umar yet laid the foundations of a democratic state, and though, owing to the peculiar conditions of the age, the principle could not be developed in all its aspects and implications, the prerequisites essential to a democratic form of government were brought into being."[18] Nevertheless, the pattern of an ideal Muslim democracy which emerges in the work of Shiblī is that of a chief executive functioning with a permanent group of advisers. This is the pattern of religio-political thought which theologians advocated in Islamic India and Pakistan during the 1940s and 1950s.

Another classical Islamic concept which has recently been equated with parliamentary democracy is that of *ijmā'* or consensus, one of the four sources of law in Islamic jurisprudence. The principle of *ijmā'* is based on the prophetic tradition, "My community will never agree upon an error." As a source of law, *ijmā'* is therefore theoretically infallible. The conception of *ijmā'* came to mean the consensus of the *'ulamā*, especially during the first two centuries of Islam. This is the traditional juristic concept of *ijmā'*.

The premodernist fundamentalist Walī-Allāh did not recognize *ijmā'* as the consensus of reasoning theologians because he believed they could never reach unanimity. He institutionalized the concept of *ijmā'* as the decision of the caliph, reached with or without the opinions of well-directed *(sāhib al-rā'y)* advisers, provided that such a decision received general approval of the community.[19] Walī-Allāh's view, though it did not foreshadow the modernist definition, was anticlassical and antitraditional and constituted a break with the past. In the traditional view it was essential that *ijmā'* should not be institutionalized and therefore as an articulate accumulation of conscience maintain its freedom from the possibility of error.[20] The modernist concept does not regard *ijmā'* as necessarily infallible, despite the prophetic tradition, and institutionalizes it not within the conceptual framework of the caliphate but within that of parliamentary democracy. In this last emphasis the modernist concept traces *ijmā'* back to its original foundations, not as the consensus of the theologians, or even of the Companions of the Prophet, but according to Shāfi'ī thought as the consensus of the entire community.[21] In the application of the concept to the modern national state, the Shāfi'īte view is modified, and the *ijmā'* is conceived as that of the people of a Muslim national state rather than that of the whole community.

Muslim modernist thought at its inception in the later nineteenth century approached the doctrine of *ijmā'* with a certain scepticism. It did not suit Sayyid Ahmad Khān as he laid the foundations of his apologetics, and he rejected it outright as a source of law. His associate and contemporary Chirāgh 'Alī concerned himself with directing his attack toward the traditional concept of the

131

consensus of theologians, pointing out that it could hardly be recognized as an infallible source of law because it was rejected by jurists like Ahmad b. Hanbal, by theologians like Ibn Hazm, and by Sūfis like Muhy al-dīn Ibn al-'Arabī.[22] Another associate of Sayyid Ahmad Khān, Muhsin al-Mulk, recognized the validity but not the infallibility of the *ijmāʿ* of the classical *'ulamā,* and saw in it the possibility of perpetual changeability.[23] Amir 'Alī regarded *ijmāʿ* as the chief and corrective source of Muslim jurisprudence and anticipated Iqbāl in his conception of it as the consensus of the people and the elite and not that of the *'ulamā.*[24]

The modernist, institutionalized concept of *ijmāʿ* begins in the subcontinent with Iqbāl. His starting point is Ibn Taymiyya's rejection of the Hanafite concept of *ijmāʿ* as understood by older legists.[25] *Ijmāʿ,* says Iqbāl, is "in my opinion, perhaps the most important legal notion in Islam. It is however strange that this important notion, while invoking great academic discussion in early Islam, remained practically a mere idea, and rarely assumed the form of a permanent institution in any Muhammedan country."[26] He continues: "It is, however, extremely satisfactory to note that the pressure of new world forces and the political experience of European nations are impressing on the mind of modern Islam the value and possibilities of the idea of *ijmāʿ.* The growth of republican spirit, and the gradual formation of legislative assemblies in Muslim lands constitutes a great step in advance. The transfer of the power of *ijtihad* from individual representatives of schools to a Muslim legislative assembly which, in view of the growth of opposing sects, is the only possible form *ijmāʿ* can take in modern times, will secure contributions to legal discussion from laymen who happen to possess a keen insight into affairs." [27] Iqbāl, however, argues with some relevance on the point of the association of *'ulamā* with a Muslim assembly or parliament of laymen, at least during the transitional stage before Muslim law is modernized.[28]

The first constitutional document of Pakistan was the Objectives Resolution passed by the first Constituent Assembly in March 1949. Its principal feature was that it regarded sovereignty as vested in God alone. The state of Pakistan through its people had been delegated authority by God to be exercised within the limits prescribed by Him. This delegation of authority was in consonance with democracy, equality, and social justice. Minorities in Pakistan were free to profess and practice their religions and develop their cultures.[29] The Objectives Resolution thus set the pattern for a compromise between the traditional Islamic concept of divine sovereignty, to which it paid lip service, and the modern concept of sovereignty, which it regarded as the delegation of a sacred trust to be exercised by the people. This compromise has been caricatured piquantly, though rather inaccurately, by Leonard Binder: "The Objectives Resolution, acknowledged the sovereignty of God, recognized the authority of the people derived from their creator, and vested the authority delegated by the people in the Constituent Assembly for the purpose of making a constitution for the sovereign state of Pakistan. Thus is God sovereign, the people sovereign, parliament sovereign, and the state sovereign in Pakistan. It would indeed be a narrow-minded person who was not satisfied with such a compromise."[30]

Though the *'ulamā* accepted the Objectives Resolution at its face value, they were not fully satisfied. Shabbīr Ahmad 'Uthmānī, discussing it in the Constituent Assembly on March 9, 1949, stated that an Islamic state must necessarily be run only by those who believed in and followed its principles. Those who did not believe in Islamic principles (presumably non-Muslims or even those who were only nominally or culturally Muslims) could be allowed to contribute to the administrative machinery of the state but could not "be entrusted with the responsibility of framing the general policy of the State or dealing with matters vital to its safety and integrity." Earlier 'Uthmānī had demanded the appointment of a committee of theologians to advise the Constituent Assembly on the requirements of an Islamic constitution. As a matter of compromise, the first and last of its kind, the government appointed such a committee of *'ulamā,* known as the Board of Islamic Teaching (Ta'līmāt-i Islāmiyya), in 1948.

The views of this board are significant for two reasons.[31] First, it constituted the only occasion when there was a recognized dia-

logue between the theologians and the Westernized political elite
on the theory and content of a constitution for Pakistan. No doubt
the constitutional commission set up in 1960 also received com-
munications from theologians and religious groups, but they were
expressions of individual and group opinion rather than official
negotiations. Second, the recommendations of the Board of Islamic Teaching, though the bulk of them were rejected as im-
practical or medieval during the process of constitution-making
from 1949 to 1962, had some influence on individual points in certain provisions in the constitutions of 1956 and 1962. The appointment of the board also represented the first occasion when the
Westernized elite tried to grasp the traditional implications of the
concept of a classical Islamic state, while the theologians on their
part showed some tempered acquiescence in accommodating modern concepts of statehood when they did not directly conflict with
the given Qur'ānic *hadīth* or juristic data. For these reasons it is
worthwhile to examine in some detail the views promulgated by
the board.

The board preferred a presidential rather than a parliamentary
system. Its recommendations concentrated on the powers and re-
sponsibilities of the head of state, most of whose qualifications
were derived from al-Māwardī's concept of a caliph. Medieval
classical theory took for granted that the caliph would be a Muslim; but this point was specifically stressed by the board and after
some discussion was accepted in all the subsequent constitutional
documents of Pakistan. On the question of tenure of office—whether for life or for a fixed period—the theologians of the board square-
ly faced the challenge of modern political ideas. Although believing
it preferable to elect the head of state for life, the board conceded
that there was nothing in the *sharīʿa* against the prescription of a
time limit. Accepting this last alternative as valid, it recommended
certain procedures to curb the chances of abuse of power by the
head of state: the right of every newly elected legislature to elect a
new leader and the unwritten convention that this person should
voluntarily submit his resignation to a new legislature after its
election, roughly once every five years.

The board asserted that "under the law of Shariat, the power to elect the Head of the State vests in the learned and pious representatives of the people," though this statement is historically inaccurate. In the context of Pakistan the board recommended that both houses of parliament "sitting together along with the Committee of Experts on Shariat should elect the Head of the State." The method it recommended as most suitable was a process of selection by elimination from a panel of qualified candidates, a procedure revivalistically modeled on the election of the third orthodox caliph 'Uthmān. The board further recommended that under certain circumstances, such as apostasy, captivity, mental derangement, or grave physical disability, the head of state could be removed from office by the legislature sitting in conjunction with the Committee of Experts on Sharī'a. There is no precedent in classical Islam for the board's further provision that a council of regency should rule during the interregnum between the deposition of one head of state and the election of the next. The council of regency was to consist of four members: the head of the supreme court, the head of the Committee of Experts on Sharī'a, and the heads of the two houses of the legislature.

Among the powers to be vested in the head of state was that of supreme commander of the armed forces. This position was adopted in the second constitution (1962), though in this case the provision must have been influenced principally by the fact that the incumbent, President Ayyūb Khān, happened to hold that office already. The board also advised that the executive powers of the state should vest in the head of state, who was to appoint his ministers in consultation with the heads of the two legislatures. The ministers were to hold office during his pleasure and could not challenge his decisions except on grounds of religious law, in which case the question was to be referred to the Committee of Experts on Sharī'a. In the event of differences of opinion between the head of state and the legislature, the question was first to be discussed in a joint session of the two houses, and then if still unresolved in a joint session of federal and provincial legislatures and their "advisory councils" (presumably the Committee of Experts on

Sharī'a). If this joint session disagreed with the head of state, the board recommended either the resignation of the head or the resolution of the question by a general referendum of the people.

The board fully accepted the principle of *shūra* but could not wholly modernize it. It regarded the Islamic government as essentially a consultative government and enjoined the head of state as chief executive to take counsel "from men of wisdom and righteousness." The board explained what it called the "fundamental difference between an absolute democratic state and an Islamic state": "In an Islamic state the implementation of the commands of Allah is the basic consideration and the will of the people occupies a comparatively subservient position; while, on the contrary, an absolute democratic state aims at the unconditional implementation of the will of the people." But any legislation not in violation of, or prejudicial to, the laws of the *sharī'a* was regarded by the board as permissible.

The board had to face the question of the position of non-Muslims in an Islamic state. The oath of office of the head of state, in the view of the board, should include a clause guaranteeing "the protection, as a Divine trust, of all the legitimate interests of non-Muslims living in Pakistan." The phraseology was vague and could be interpreted either liberally or conservatively, but the emphasis on divine trust is presumably derived from a policy attributed to 'Umar.[32]

The board believed that women should not sit in the legislature, but if their election was found to be unavoidable under modern circumstances, it suggested two conditions of eligibility: women legislators should have attained the age of fifty and they should observe purdah (veiling). Under no circumstances, the board held, could a woman be elected as head of state.

The lower house of parliament (House of the People) was equated by the board with the classical *majlis al-hall wa'l-'aqd*, with powers to elect or depose the head of state, to deal with differences of opinion between the head and itself, and to watch over the activities of the executive. The lower house also was to have the powers of declaring war, concluding peace treaties, and approving the national budget. The board later contradicted itself and revealed its inexperience in politics and its inconsistency in political thinking by equating this very classical concept of the *majlis al-hall wa'l-'aqd* with a "larger representative body," which was more a vast electoral college for selecting the legislature than the legislature itself. Whereas the legislature might include non-Muslims, the electoral college was to consist of Muslims conversant with *sharī'a*. In elections to the legislature the board recommended that the conditions of election of non-Muslims be the same as those for Muslims, but with the addition of a clause outlining a criterion of their loyalty.

The Constituent Assembly's subcommittee on federal and provincial constitutions and distribution of powers questioned the board's ruling that the head of state should be a Muslim. In its reply the board upheld its position emphatically, quoting rather questionably a number of Qur'ānic verses, as well as instances from the constitutions of a number of Muslim and non-Muslim states which provided that the head of state should be of the same religious persuasion as the majority of its people. On this one point, it should be said, the board exercised a lasting and final influence on Pakistan's constitution-making. And Pakistan's weakness on this point was in a sense later exploited by India when it elected Zākir Husayn, a Muslim, as its president in 1967.

One further aspect of the board's views on the position of non-Muslims is worth noting. In response to criticism of its preference for a presidential system, the board protested that it "could not feel convinced that our present needs of the country or of the Millat [national community] were really such as to make it indispensable or even preferable to adopt the Parliamentary system"; if, however, this system was absolutely indispensable, it could be adopted only on condition that all members of the legislature "must necessarily be Muslims possessing the requisite qualifications."

The views of the board thus constitute the traditional conception of an Islamic state with certain concessions to modernization. The only other significant blueprint of an Islamic state and of the position of democracy in it was formulated over a number of years by the fundamentalist, Mawdūdī. His position is based on an externalist interpretation of the Qur'ān; and though he pays lip service to the juristic development of Islamic law, unlike the traditionalists he does not use it as a basic source for his religious or political theories.

Mawdūdī's political thought differs from that of the traditionalists particularly on the point of the role of the head of state. Mawdūdī does not insist in theory on the Islamic state being run on the presidential system. He is satisfied on the whole with a parliamentary system in which man acts as the agent of the sovereign God and democracy is, in fact, "theo-democracy." Although Mawdūdī gave currency to this expression, the term was probably first used by a conservative-minded modernist, 'Umar Hayāt Malik, as early as 1949.[33] The theo-democracy of Mawdūdī's conception is to be run by a party of pious, strictly conformist Muslims, who would control it in much the same way that a fascist government controls a totalitarian state.[34] Mawdūdī in fact created a political party, the Jamā'at-i Islamī, with this program in view. According to Mawdūdī ultimate legal and constitutional authority vests in God, and man is allowed a measure of freedom of choice strictly circumscribed by the Revelation. If a Muslim society decides to base its constitution on borrowed legal or constitutional elements, it ceases to be Islamic. The *sharī'a* as revealed in the Qur'ān is an organic whole and cannot be applied to a state or society in bits and pieces.[35] Islamic laws are eternal and for all time; they cannot become antiquated or out of date.

All the same, like the modernists Mawdūdī sees in the classical concepts of *shūra* and *ijmā'* the elements of a modern parliamentary system.[36] This parliamentary system is to be controlled by the party of the pious Islamic elite, who in turn must conform strictly to the discipline imposed by an elected chief or *amīr*.[37] In theory Mawdūdī does not equate this *amīr* with the head of state, though such a chief would actually possess great power, much like the secretary of the Communist party in a Communist state. Mawdūdī's theoretical position has been that no woman can be elected head of state, but with the opportunism which has characterized his political party he supported Miss Fātimah Jinnāh against President Ayyūb Khān in the presidential elections of 1963.

As regards non-Muslims, Mawdūdī's view is that they should have equality with Muslims in civil and criminal law and be allowed to apply their own personal law. But they cannot be permitted to worship publicly in "Muslim" cities nor to build or repair temples and churches, as they are allowed to do in classical theory. No non-Muslim can serve as head of state, hold a key position in the administration, or be a member of parliament. But non-Muslims would be permitted to propose codifications and amendments of their own personal law. Finally Mawdūdī insists that they must pay *jizya* (a tax on non-Muslims) and must be debarred from defense services.

The question then arises, to what extent did the traditionalist and fundamentalist theories of a political system actually affect the growth of Pakistan as a modern, and to some qualified extent, a democratic state? The answer is that some of the views of the theologians of both varieties—with the notable exception of their attitude to non-Muslims—were, as theories, absorbed or adopted with mental reservations in the constitutional documents. However, in practice the administrations of the First Republic, the martial law regime, and the Second Republic have resisted these theories and attempted to mold Pakistan along the lines of a modern national state.

Democracy in the Western sense was first subverted by Ghulām Muhammad, the governor-general who dismissed the cabinet headed by Khwajā Nāzim al-dīn in 1953 and who dissolved the first Constituent Assembly in 1954 when it legislated to curtail the powers of the governor-general. These actions of Ghulām Ahmad were motivated by a quest for efficiency in administration as well as by such undesirable traits as provincialism and personal ambition. He drew his support from the civil service, and his actions had no religious overtones. The ad hoc election of the second Constituent Assembly in 1955 was again based on a secular origin, the ruling of the supreme court of Pakistan on the constitutional dispute

139

which arose out of the dismissal of the first assembly. From 1955 onward Iskandar Mirza, a civil servant who entered the political arena as a minister and who became governor-general and president, raised the slogan of "controlled democracy." This occurred as interregional rivalries and the personal ambitions of politicians turned the parliamentary system into chaos. Here again was a secular slogan. It influenced the thinking of President Ayyūb Khān and his advisers in the creation of a partly elective system of union councils at the basic village and urban levels and indirect elections through them. This system of "basic democracies," as they are popularly called, is modeled on the pre-Islamic, ancient Indian *panchāyat* system which was revived by the British, although some persons have claimed an Islamic ancestry for it. As a matter of fact, in theory as in practice, the entire concept and structure of the basic democracies is purely secular.

Finally the authoritarian regime of the military revolution from 1958 to 1962 and the presidential system of democracy from 1962 onward is a secular development, like similar revolutions and similar political systems in many countries of Asia and Africa, Muslim as well as non-Muslim. The presidential system as crystallized in theory in the second constitution and as realized in practice in the second republic, is a purely political development, and any resemblances it may have with the recommendations of the Board of Islamic Teaching are coincidental rather than actual.

Indeed as early as 1954 Ayyūb Khān raised questions about the lack of a proper definition of Islamic democracy: "Would it . . . not be correct to say that any variety of democracy when worked in the spirit of the Qur'an can be called an Islamic Democracy?" Though in one context he regarded his own presidential cabinet as modeled on the pattern of the caliphal *shūra,* he observed that in the orthodox caliphate "no specific pattern of government or even of the election of the Head of Government had been established. The conclusion was inescapable that Islam had not prescribed any particular pattern of government but had left it to the community to evolve its own pattern to suit its circumstances, provided that the principles of the Qur'an and the Sunnah were observed."[88]

REFERENCES

1. Muhammad Miyān, *'Ulamā-i Haqq awr unkē mujāhidāna kārnāme* (Delhi, 1946), 1:100. For an English translation of the injunction see Hafeez Malik, *Moslem Nationalism in India and Pakistan* (Washington, D.C., 1963), p. 196.

2. Mahmūd al-Hasan, "Presidential Address," Jam'iyyat al-'ulamā-i Hind, Delhi, 1920, cited in Husayn Ahmad Madanī, *Naqsh-i Hayāt* (Delhi, 1953), 1:191–92; see also 2:253–55, 259.

3. Iqbāl, *Struggle for Independence* (Karachi, 1957), pp. 15–16.

4. *Ibid.*, p. 34.

5. *Proceedings of the Joint Committee on Indian Constitutional Reform, 1934*, vol. 1, pt. 1, pp. 11–26; C. H. Philips, *Evolution of India and Pakistan 1858–1947* (London, 1962), p. 308.

6. Jamil-ud-Din Ahmed, ed., *Speeches and Writings of Mr. Jinnah* (Lahore, 1952), 1: 117.

7. G. E. von Grünebaum, *Modern Islam* (Berkeley, 1962), p. 81.

8. Qur'ān 48:18. In Arberry's version: "God was well pleased with the believers when they were swearing fealty to thee under the tree, and He knew what was in their hearts, so He sent down the Shechina upon them, and rewarded them with a nigh victory and many spoils to take; and God is ever All-mighty, All-wise."

9. Qur'ān 42:36.

10. Gibb, "Constitutional Development," in M. Khadduri and H. J. Liebesny, eds., *Law in the Middle East* (Washington, D.C., 1955), p. 16.

11. Shāh Walī-Allāh, *Izāla al-khafā* (Urdu tr.; Karachi, n.d.), 1: 470.

12. Ahmad Jevdet, *Vaqā'i Devlet-i 'Aliye* (Istanbul, 1855), 9: 3–7, 338–39; Niyazi Berkes, *The Development of Secularism in Turkey* (Montreal, 1964), p. 90.

13. 'Abd al-Rahmān al-Rāfi'ī, *Asr Muhammad 'Alī* (Cairo, 1951), pp. 608–10, 613–14.

14. Reşat Kaynar, *Mustafa Reşit Paşa ve Tanzimat* (Ankara, 1954), pp. 172–73; Berkes, *Development of Secularism in Turkey*, p. 145.

15. 'Abd al-Rahmān al-Rāfi'ī, *'Asr Ismā'īl* (Cairo, 1948), 2:78 and *passim*.

16. Serif Mardin, *The Genesis of Young Ottoman Thought* (Princeton, 1962), pp. 292–93. I am grateful to my colleagues Professors E. Kuran and L. Kenny for their assistance in tracing the early uses of the terms *shūra* and *meshveret*. See also the contributions by Bernard Lewis and Majid Khadduri under "Dustūr" in *Encyclopaedia of Islam*, 2nd ed., 2 (1965): 640–47, 647–49.

17. M. Shiblī Nu'mānī, *'Umar the Great* (Lahore, 1947–57), 2:16; he gives the name of some "permanent members" of 'Umar's "consultative assembly" on the authority of Ibn Sa'd, *Tabaqāt* (Hyderabad), 3: 134.

18. Shiblī Nu'mānī, *al-Fārūq*, 2:16.

19. Shāh Walī-Allāh, *Izāla*, 1: 72, 262.

20. Cf. Malcolm H. Kerr, *Islamic Reform* (Berkeley and Los Angeles, 1966), pp. 79–80.

21. For a discussion of the various classical and modern theories of *ijmā'* see George Hourani, "The Basis of Authority of Consensus in Sunnite Islam," *Studia Islamica*, 21 (1964): 13–60.

22. Chirāgh 'Alī (Cheragh Ali), *The Proposed Political, Legal and Social Reforms in the Ottoman Empire and Other Mohammedan States* (Bombay, 1883).

23. Muhsin al-Mulk in *Tahdhīb al-akhlāq* (collected reprint; Lahore, n.d.), 1: 68–69, 159–62.

141

24. Amīr 'Alī (Ameer Ali), *The Spirit of Islam* (London, 1961), p. 251. For the concept of *ijmā'* in modern Indian Islam, see Aziz Ahmad, *Islamic Modernism in India and Pakistan, 1857–1964* (London, 1967), pp. 54, 60, 70, 96, 154–55, and *passim*.

25. Muhammad Iqbāl, *The Reconstruction of Religious Thought in Islam* (Lahore, 1944), p. 152.

26. *Ibid.*, p. 173.

27. *Ibid.*, p. 173.

28. *Ibid.*, p. 175–76.

29. Pakistan, *Constituent Assembly Debates*, v/1 (March 7, 1949).

30. Binder, *Religion and Politics in Pakistan* (Berkeley, 1961), p. 149.

31. "Views of the Board of Ta'līmāt-i Islāmiyya on Certain Items Referred to Them by the Sub-Committee on Federal and Provincial Constitutions and Distribution of Powers," printed as Appendix I of Pakistan, *Report of the Sub-Committee on Federal and Provincial Constitutions and Distribution of Powers* (Karachi, 1950); reprinted in Binder, *Religion and Politics in Pakistan*, pp. 383–429.

32. Cf. 'Umar to Sa'd b. Abū Waggās, in Nuwayrī, *Nihāyat al-'arab*, 6:168–69; cf. also at-Tabarī, *Annals* (Leiden: de Goeje, 1871), 4:211, 212.

33. Pakistan, *Constituent Assembly Debates*, v/5 (March 12, 1949), p. 78.

34. Manfred Halpern, *The Politics of Social Change in the Middle East and North Africa* (Princeton, 1963), pp. 134, 150–51; Aziz Ahmad, "Mawdūdī and Orthodox Fundamentalism in Pakistan," *Middle East Journal*, 21 (1967): 369–80; Freeland Abbott, "The Jama'at-i-Islami of Pakistan," *Middle East Journal*, 11 (1957): 37–51.

35. Abul Ala Maududi (Abu'l A'lā Mawdūdī), *Islamic Law and Constitution* (Lahore, 1960), pp. 47–48, 50–54.

36. *Ibid.*, pp. 85–95.

37. Mawdūdī, *Musalmān awr mawjūda siyāsī kashmakash* (Pathankot, 1937–39), 3:101–12, 171–84.

38. Mohammad Ayub Khan, *Friends Not Masters: A Political Autobiography* (London, 1967), pp. 190, 198.

} ROBERT R. JAY {

History and Personal Experience · Religious and Political Conflict in Java

Toward the end of 1965 widespread massacres broke out in Indonesia, and hundreds of thousands of persons died because they could be in some way identified with the left wing. The massacres were especially intense in Java, where conservative estimates of the deaths run upward to half a million. The purpose of this paper is to consider the nature of this event, first as a short violent segment of a long historical process, and second within a frame of personal experience. The aim, beyond explicating the event, is to assess the kind of knowledge that comes to us through each mode of viewing.[1]

To view historically is to seek to understand the bearing on particular events of some of their particular antecedents. The view does not necessarily assume causality between them, but it does assume that there is some consistency in the flow of events, that patterns appearing earlier will be recognizable, though perhaps unpredictably modified, in a later period, and that what may emerge later will reflect light upon what has happened earlier. In this way a succession of modified patterns can be sorted out of one historical sequence and taken as a single strand of process. The first part of this paper attempts to establish such a strand of process in Javanese history, one which passes through the events of the massacres. It is important to understand that the process, as a perceived regularity, consists of patterns evident in events, not of the events themselves. Any event comprises much more than just such patterns; no single process, nor all the processes evident in an event taken together, can definitively explain that event, in the sense of exhausting its meaning for us. The second part of the paper seeks to discover the meaning the event can have as human experience and to show that we gain a different kind of knowledge of the event when it is so viewed.

For reasons of economy the discussion has been limited principally to a historical process which emerged in Java. Different processes related to the same general factors — the interaction of Islam and preexisting systems of religion and politics — appeared elsewhere in Indonesia, but despite some congruence with the patterning of this process in Java, they cannot be treated as simple variants of the Javanese case and are not considered here.

In tracing the line of process I am interested in, I begin rather arbitrarily with the initial conversion of the Javanese states to Islam, roughly from 1300 A.D. to 1525 A.D. The period coincides with the rise and decline of the last and most illustrious pre-Muslim Javanese kingdom, Madjapahit. During that time significant conversion to Islam among the Hinduized ruling classes of the Javanese states seems to have taken place through the influence of Indian Muslim traders. Overseas trade was one of the main sources of Madjapahit's wealth and power, and important state offices were given to foreign traders as a way of improving the efficiency of the state's relations with the overseas trading sector. With the conversion of most Indian states to Islam after the Muslim conquests of the eleventh and twelfth centuries, the foreign-trade sector of East Indian society became increasingly dominated by Muslim elements.

The earliest evidence for such influences in Madjapahit is the presence of a Muslim burial ground, with some tombstones bearing dates between 1376 and 1475 A.D., located in the immediate vicinity of what is probably the site of the Madjapahit royal palace. The style of the tombs shows a fusion of Javanese and Islamic forms and seems to indicate that a Muslim community, at least partly Javanized and well connected with the Madjapahit royal court, existed during the great flowering of that Hindu-Javanese kingdom.

The fifteenth and sixteenth centuries saw a considerable increase in trade between the Far East, India, the Near East, and Europe, and those Javanese involved in overseas trade became more and more powerful. By the middle of the fifteenth century at least, trading states in the western part of the Indies — along the coasts of Borneo, Malaya, and Sumatra, including the overseas colonies of Javanese traders — were asserting their independence of Madjapahit. The local rulers of harbor states along the north coast of Java, who had mostly gained their positions as regents of the Madjapahit ruler and who were deeply involved in overseas trade, also became increasingly independent of the central government. And it was among these rulers, as among the overseas trading colonies, that Muslim influences on the Javanese ruling class were most powerful and that conversions to Islam gained the most ground. Adherence to Islam came to be joined to pressures for political independence from the Hinduist Madjapahit ruler, each influence mutually identifying and reinforcing the other.

The north-coast harbor states in Java were able to defend their claims to independence and finally to carry the attack against Madjapahit itself. By the early part of the sixteenth century, around 1520 according to various traditional Javanese histories, a coalition of harbor states led by the Sultan of Demak overthrew the last Madjapahit ruler and carried off to Demak the royal regalia. There followed a period of some seventy-five years during which a kind of confederacy of Muslimized harbor states controlled increasingly large areas of Java, converting local states to Islam as their power expanded. Overseas trade expanded too, although by this time Portugal had entered the area as an active, highly belligerent participant, operating from its base at Malacca, which it had conquered in 1511.

These years were certainly important for the establishment of Islam in Java. They were years of absorption, fusion, and differentiation. Literature and music, as well as religious ritual and thought from India, entered through the overseas gates of the north Javanese trading ports (though that is not to say that no such material had come in during the Madjapahit period). Variant modes of *wayang*, the traditional Javanese shadow puppet theater that uses tales based on the Hindu epics of the Mahabharata and Ramayana, were created for adaptation to Muslimized Indian and Persian tales. Dance, chants, and drum music, in part probably brought along with Sufi modes of Islamic worship, were grafted onto traditional Javanese poetry. Geometric and floral design replaced much Hindu-Javanese pictorial design. There were changes in the political and judicial systems toward accommodating Muslim legal theory, as well of course as sharp changes in the relation between the state and the religious establishments. The early political leaders of the Muslimized harbor states were themselves viewed as Muslim holy men and religious teachers. They resisted as heresy, however, the standard religious theory of the Hindu-Buddhist period which identified the ruler with the divine. A council of them went so far as to condemn one of their number, Sheik Siti Djenar, to be burned alive for teaching a version of Islam which identified the self with the divine.

We can only infer the kinds of antagonisms which the turnover of religious and political power during this period may have aroused or reinforced within Javanese society. The Hindu and Buddhist ceremonial centers were abandoned by the state (though not necessarily by the local communities). The political theology of Islam, according to which the ruler is a human "defender of the faith," formally replaced the traditional, highly elaborated Javanese theology by which the ruler, fixed in his palace center — the concrete manifestation of the mystical axis of the universe — is the central mediator between man and the divine forces. The *Djaman Dewa*, or *Djaman Buda*, the "era of the gods," gave way to the *Djaman Islam*. Court philosophers and religious leaders turned to Koranic and other Near Eastern literary and philosophical works as sources for traditional histories, moral inquiries, poetry, and literary entertainments. The new powers stressed maritime interests and trade, rather than the control of the manpower and production of the rural countryside through elaborate religious and secular hierarchies. Families with hereditary rights to positions in the Madjapahit bureaucracy were reduced to insignificance as power and population shifted away from the interior, especially of eastern Java, toward the seaports.

Near the end of the sixteenth century a new center of political power emerged in inland central Java, in the area of present-day Jogjakarta and Surakarta. This area, Mataram, had been one of the first locales for the development of Javanese civilization during the seventh and eighth centuries. Fertile and easily irrigable, it supported a large population and was the center of political power in Java until the tenth century. Then, for reasons not well understood, the area became depopulated and political power shifted to eastern Java; during the Madjapahit period it was a border province of small significance. But in 1585 a new, independent kingdom was established there, retaining the name of Mataram. Its very establishment was a challenge to the harbor states of the north coast, and warfare soon developed between the two power centers.

The records of Mataram's growth and its struggles with the coastal states dominated by orthodox Islam provide the first clear view of the political and religious schism between orthodox and syncretist Muslims in Java. The early rulers of Mataram seem deliberately to have set about restoring numerous religious and political elements from the Madjapahit period. Royal officials were recruited from the Madjapahit families of officials and aristocrats, dispossessed but still presumably conscious of their hereditary power. Traditional Hindu-Javanese learning and state ritual were reinstated at the Mataram court. Accommodation to Islam was reduced to certain formal observances, and although the state remained formally Islamic and no reinstatement of Hindu or Buddhist religious offices occurred, many conceptions linking the ruler as a semidivine to his deceased forebears and to the general populace were ritually reaffirmed and reinforced in the society. The

147

Mataram rulers set about establishing their office as "king of the mountain" in Java, a traditional ruling effort which the north-coast rulers of orthodox inclination had not attempted.

Court scholars in Mataram developed a literary and religious synthesis of traditional Javanese and Muslim elements that yielded very little indeed to the latter. The character of their efforts is well illustrated by the following extract from one version of the *Babad Tanah Djawi*, a reworked history of Java produced in various editions at the Mataram court during the reigns of the earlier rulers.

This is the history of the kings of Java, beginning with the Prophet Adam, who had a son Sis. Sis had a son Nurtjahja [Sanskrit: sacred primal light]. Nurtjahja had a son Nurasa [primal feeling, sensing]. Nurasa had a son Sanghjang Wening [divine, clear fluid]. Sanghjang Wening had a son Sanghjang Tunggal [divine unity]. Sanghjang Tunggal had a son Batara Guru [synonym for Siwa]. Batara Guru had five children, named Batara Sambo, Batara Brama, Batara Mahadewa, Batara Wisnu, and Dewi Sri [Javanese goddess of rice]. Batara Wisnu was king on the island of Java under the name of Prabhu Set. The kingdom of Batara Guru was called Sura-Laja [Hindu paradise].

The history then goes on to describe quarrels between Batara Wisnu and his father Batara Guru and to draw genealogical lines from these figures, especially Brama and Wisnu, to the various historical kings of Java. The whole preface is plainly inspired by Hindu-Javanese creation myths, with slight deference paid to Islamic conceptions.

This kind of religious syncretism shocked the more orthodox of the Javanese political and religious leaders and it lent a strong religious coloration to the political rivalry between Mataram and the north-coast harbor states. The harbor rulers invoked the purity of an orthodox Islam against the Mataram rulers and encouraged religious teachers to preach against the Mataram court. The Mataram rulers waged all-out war against the harbor states, during which much of east Java was depopulated, and they suppressed orthodox teachers, at times slaying them in large numbers. The first stage of the struggle between Mataram and the northeast coast ended when Mataram destroyed the port of Surabaya in 1625, following the conquest of the other harbor states. All the ports were closed to overseas trade except for one, which was allowed to operate only under strict control of the Mataram government. The Mataram rulers seemed determined not to suffer the same fate as Madjapahit.

Rebellion and war followed again and again in the east of Java, most especially in 1675 and again in 1718. Each time the Mataram rulers were able to put down the rebellion, though only by drawing on help from the Dutch East Indies Company, by then firmly established on the coast of west Java. In each case Mataram had to yield up sovereignty to the Dutch company over wide areas of central Java. Finally in 1825 central Java was shaken by a convulsive revolution under the leadership of Dipanegara, an aristocratic but markedly orthodox member of the ruling family. The revolution was directed as much against the Dutch as against the Mataram rulers, for by this time Dutch power and influence had penetrated deeply into Javanese society and was serving to control and prop up the throne. Only after five years of hard fighting, much of it guerrilla warfare, were the Dutch able to subdue the rebels and capture Dipanegara.

With the end of the war the Dutch took over effective administration of the whole of Java. They carried forward, in more organized form, their earlier policy of "indirect rule," under which local administration was largely left in the hands of Javanese "regents" recruited from local families with strong bureaucratic ties to the Javanese court. The regents were directly responsible to Dutch territorial officials, termed "controlleurs," who had the power of dismissal over them. Lower officials were all Javanese, recruited through the same ties of family and court preference. In this way the pre-Dutch Mataram bureaucracy was carried forward largely intact, more thoroughly organized, and even more thoroughly hereditary. Over a period of time Dutch-staffed positions were thrust farther down into the territorial administration and the bureaucratic positions filled by Javanese were expanded and rationalized, yet the ideological attitudes of the Javanese officialdom

149

continued the inheritance from Mataram — traditional Javanism in philosophy and the arts, and antagonistic to orthodox Islam.

During the rest of the nineteenth century and into the twentieth, local revolts against officialdom, similar to the conflict of 1825 but much smaller in scope, continued to occur all over Java. At a village in eastern Java I visited a local shrine, venerated by the villagers as one of their points of access to spiritual blessings, which was the grave of the leader of one such small rebellion. According to the village account, he was an orthodox religious teacher who had become embroiled in a fight over land rights with local government officials and had killed one of them. He next routed a small force of government police sent to investigate and then, refusing to answer the summons of the local regent, defeated and killed the regent in battle. He had by that time gained a considerable body of followers. Not until the Dutch sent in a military force was the rebellion broken and its leader killed. Birds, the villagers said, fell dead if they flew over his grave.

Such incidents took place in the countryside, not in towns or cities, and their characteristic form — a gathering about a charismatic leader able to promise mystical weapons and support — follows modes of religious thought and organization common in rural Javanese society.[2] More frequent intercourse of Javanese Muslims with Mecca during the latter part of the nineteenth century augmented the strength of orthodoxy and the power of orthodox leaders in rural society, as well as increasing the antagonism toward the Dutch colonial regime. Such local rural movements, however, were transitory and unconnected, and did not lead to a genuine nationalist movement, which began only with the development of organizations in urban Javanese society early in the twentieth century.

The first major political organization to emerge among urban Javanese was again based on the appeal of orthodox Islam as against the Javanese bureaucracy and European power. The movement started in 1912 as a small association of Javanese Muslim traders who united to provide mutual support especially against Chinese traders. Under the name Sarekat Islam, the organization quickly expanded its mission and appeal into a program for the religious and material betterment of all the Muslims of the Dutch East Indies (which the program equated with virtually all its indigenous peoples). The response in Java was impressive. Within three years the organization had grown into a mass movement with numerous branches in the major Javanese cities, many towns, and even some villages.

Sarekat Islam directed its action against Christianity, Dutch rule, and the Javanese aristocracy as sources of defilement of Islam and of degeneration of the native peoples in the Indies. It thus raised itself against orthodox Islam's old rivals in Java, but its very success brought into it new social elements from within Javanese society that turned out to be more dangerous than its traditional enemies.

As early as 1915 the Dutch leader of a radical socialist party in the Indies had encouraged young Javanese political organizers to enter Sarekat Islam in order to orient it toward the international left. The young radicals attracted small urban artisans and laborers and were strikingly effective at establishing labor unions. Under their pressure the Sarekat Islam leadership increasingly shifted its politics toward more radical anticapitalist and anticolonialist positions. At the same time, however, the orthodox leaders worked to spread a modernist version of orthodoxy, including action in support of international Pan-Islam, through the vehicle of Sarekat Islam. Indeed the leadership of each group, the left wing and the orthodox, assumed that its message was complementary to and not competitive with that of the other. Ingenious efforts were made to equate communism with Islam and vice versa. International communism was identified with the Mahdi, the Islamic messiah, whose coming would establish a just and prosperous state, while Western capitalism was identified with the Islamic equivalent of the anti-Christ.

To the apparent surprise of both parties, the essential antagonism between such exclusivist world ideologies as Islam and communism frustrated these naïve efforts at accommodation, and at the annual congress of Sarekat Islam in 1921 the orthodox wing succeeded in forcing an issue which led the left-wing branches to withdraw as an organizational unit, though for a time they retained their identity as Sarekat Islam branches. The division, it turned out, was roughly fifty-fifty, an indication of the left wing's attractiveness to Javanese urban dwellers. From that time until the dissolution in 1926 of the Indonesian Communist party and of its suspected affiliates (including the left-wing branches of Sarekat Islam), the orthodox leaders remaining in Sarekat Islam explored and developed anti-Communist, antisecular lines of argument, while the left-wing leaders similarly developed antiorthodox positions. Neither succeeded in making inroads into the political territory of the other, but they did manage to begin the process by which the organizational scopes of the left and of orthodoxy in Javanese society were to reach mutual exclusion.

In the vacuum created by the dissolution of the Communist party in 1926, the orthodox leadership of Sarekat Islam tried to carry on organizing activities in the labor-union field, using left-wing socialist appeals in its oratory (so far as it dared in face of the suspicions of the Dutch colonial government). It had small success, for such appeals, linked as they were with orthodox religious figures and messages, apparently aroused no enthusiasm among people earlier stirred by the left wing's own appeal. After 1926 the organizational power and scope of Sarekat Islam contracted to those persons in each branch community who were strongly orthodox and reformist, as well as politically minded.

Sarekat Islam's organizational failure was not due simply to the conservative reaction which followed the suppression of left-wing organizations and their members. Late in the 1920s there appeared on the political scene new nationalist political movements led by certain young urban intellectuals, most notably Sukarno. These groups, wholly secular in their appeal, entered into competition with Sarekat Islam by taking antiorthodox positions on issues concerning the development of Indonesian society and nationalist strategy (such as attacks on polygamy and the easy divorce allowed men by Islamic law, and on Pan-Islamic efforts). These secular-oriented nationalist parties received a much quicker and more enthusiastic response than Sarekat Islam, so much so that Sukarno and his colleagues were put on trial for their inflammatory message and imprisoned in New Guinea. Their successors continued as best they dared, organizing more or less radical political groupings that were always nonorthodox, at times even aggressively antiorthodox in tone, and that more successfully than any orthodox political group carried the ideological message of Indonesian nationalism to the public during the prewar years.

During the wartime occupation of Indonesia by the Japanese, important organizational amalgamations took place among the various nationalist movements, and the Japanese stimulated, even enforced, much new organization in both urban and rural society. As part of an appeal to Islam for support against the Western powers, the Japanese gave orthodox Islamic groups a single, over-all organization with considerable autonomy, and by the end of the occupation they had achieved a separate department of religious affairs in the government, much to the horror of the nonorthodox groups. The nonorthodox organizations were similarly grouped under a single tent under the leadership of Sukarno (by then released from New Guinea), with more governmental responsibility than the orthodox union and correspondingly less autonomy. With the fall of Japan these two organizational blocks emerged as the most politically powerful elements in the new nation of Indonesia. Various nonaffiliated groups sprang up beside them, most importantly the Indonesian Communist party, which emerged from under ground.

At the same time multitudes of guerrilla units began to crystallize all over the Javanese landscape, imbued with a sense of mission and protest created by the declaration of Indonesian independence on August 17, 1945, and by the expanding beachheads of Allied troops landed to secure the surrender of the Japanese military forces. The guerrilla bands coalesced around all sorts of groups, formal and informal: the National Defense Militia (which became the Indonesian army), Japanese-trained paramilitary groups, rural Muslim boarding schools, high schools, and even local urban neighborhoods. A specialized study of the period by John

Smail clearly describes how such groups grew, organized, armed, and affiliated themselves with one or another larger organization.[3]

In this fashion the various political organizations, new and old (and all organizations were then politically active on the issues of the revolution), strove to attract bands of guerrilla adherents, though such affiliations were often very unstable. Gradually more and more of the bands shifted their loyalties to the larger, better-organized military groups, mostly to the Indonesian national army; yet many, while doing so, tried to retain their own political identification and above all their own leadership; similarly the leaders tried to retain the loyalty of their followers through such identification. In particular those bands which identified themselves with radical left-wing positions, as well as those which identified themselves with orthodox Islam, made strong efforts to maintain their own cohesiveness.

The national leaders of the new Indonesian army, some with prewar officer-training in the Dutch forces, were generally non-radical and pragmatic in their approach to military organization. Politically they were moderates and generally unsympathetic to the left. They worked steadily to organize the army's structure along conventional military lines, to maximize coordination, and to reduce cores of independent power within the army. Left-wing military leaders, younger and lacking in seniority, felt themselves gravely threatened when senior officers at the general staff level attempted to break up their units and redistribute them among other more politically stable units, all in the name of military efficiency. The left-wingers felt, perhaps correctly, that these moves were in fact aimed at eliminating Communist military strength.

This situation seems to have been the most powerful factor in setting off the bloody Madiun Affair of September 1948. Various Communist-oriented military units seized power in their areas of operation and called for a general uprising that would overthrow the "Fascist" government of Sukarno and Mohammad Hatta (then the republic's president and vice-president respectively) and establish a "People's Democracy" in its place. After several weeks of bitter civil war, mainly around the left-wing stronghold of Madiun in east Java, Republican forces succeeded in suppressing the rebels and restoring their own authority. During that time, however, the civil war opened up a dreadful and, to the Javanese, totally unexpected fissure in local society. Those who became partisans on the left not only turned violently upon officeholders of the Republican government but also struck with extraordinary viciousness in the towns and across the countryside against influential orthodox persons, especially religious teachers and their students. Orthodox groups struck back, not simply at Communist partisans but also at anyone believed to be a Communist collaborator or sympathizer. This often turned out to mean any strongly nonorthodox person. According to official accounts half the adult males caught inside Ponorogo, a city of 50,000 to the south of Madiun, were killed by one side or the other.

In the rural area of central eastern Java which I visited in 1953–54, I was told that the local orthodox communities, when they learned about the bloodshed in the Madiun district, immediately raised militia and invaded adjacent nonorthodox, syncretist-oriented communities. There they killed persons suspected of Communist activities and forced community leaders to conform to orthodox religious ritual, including attendance at the mosques of the orthodox communities. One of the orthodox villagers explained their action this way:

It was like this, Mas. We began hearing the news from Madiun. Religious teachers and their students were shut up in their schools and their buildings burned down. They had done nothing, these were old men with gray hair, good men, and boys. It was just because they were Muslims. People were taken out into the city square, in front of the mosque, and their heads were cut off. The gutters of the streets there were three centimeters deep with blood, Mas. When we heard these things here, we could not bear it, we had to do something.

In my village national army men arrived quickly to put an end to the fighting and persuade the orthodox militia to return home. Elsewhere in the area, however, there was bloodshed, though not on the scale of the terror around Madiun.

Left-wing military strength was broken as a result of the Mad-

iun Affair, but in 1952, after peace and independence had been
secured, the Communist party was allowed to reorganize politically and proceeded to do so with swift, even fantastic, success. By
1953, in the rural community in which I stayed, the party was
busily and successfully establishing local branches of national Boy
Scout, youth, farmer, and women's associations — even a branch
of an organization to reclaim traditional Javanese learning for the
nation. In the national parliamentary elections of 1955 and 1956
the Communists emerged as one of the four major parties, and in
local municipal elections thereafter they very often came out on
top.

In their campaigning the Communist party and its affiliates regu-
larly identified themselves as champions of nonorthodoxy, and in
my area it was in the nonorthodox communities, especially those
oriented strongly toward traditional Javanese culture, that their
appeal was most effective. Conversely they failed to organize in
any orthodox community. Their organizational success in syncretist communities greatly increased the cultural frictions between orthodox and nonorthodox communities, already tender
from earlier and continuing orthodox campaigning. The wildfire
surge of Communist organization in the countryside where I
stayed certainly gained much of its power from that cultural antagonism and in turn fed it; apparently the same factors were
working elsewhere in Java.

Nationally the Communist party worked toward a respectable
political alliance with President Sukarno and sympathetically
minded politicians of the other major nonorthodox political group,
the Nationalist party. The Communists were again highly successful and by 1957 had emerged as the most solidly organized and politically effective party in Indonesia. Left-wing pressures on the
conduct of foreign affairs, on many government departments, on
the press and other mass media, and on writers and artists either
eliminated or aligned with the left thousands of influential government officials, politicians, merchants (especially among the Chinese), and intellectuals. As a result Indonesia's international
course veered sharply leftward. In 1958 the miserable failure of an

anti-Sukarno military rebellion, centered in Sumatra and the Celebes and largely led by important orthodox Muslim military and political leaders, led to the banning of the Masjumi party, the Communist party's major orthodox rival. This left the Communists and their affiliates as the strongest and best organized political grouping in the nation, matched in power only by the army.

President Sukarno's relations with the army were close and important for both. After 1950 the government took a parliamentary form, with administration in the hands of a prime minister and cabinet directly responsible to the parliament. The many parties represented and the complexity of their relations produced frequent changes of cabinet. Sukarno's position as titular commander-in-chief of the armed forces gave him important leverage in the factional struggles for control particularly within the army, amorphous and loosely knit as it was after the revolution. This leverage Sukarno used to increase his political power vis-à-vis the parliament. Contending army leaders, generally scornful of party politicians, sided with him against parliament, and his alliance with the left wing gave him further important strength among influential intellectuals and the press. When in July 1959 Sukarno dissolved the existing parliament, banned political parties from the governing process, and ruled directly through his own conception of government, "Guided Democracy," there was no one left with the political strength to protest nor any open forum to protest from.

In subsequent years the competition between the army and the Communist party became steadily more intense, and President Sukarno found it increasingly difficult to maintain a balance between them. Under this pressure and in response to his own visions of national development, he shifted slowly leftward. For a time — from 1959 to 1962, when the problem was settled in favor of Indonesia — the issue of Indonesian versus Dutch sovereignty over western New Guinea gave him a popular issue for uniting both sides; later the confrontation with Malaysia over its attempt to admit the northern Borneo states then under British control similarly served him for a while. By 1965, however, confrontation had lost its dramatic edge and settled into stalemate. Sukarno's response was to swing still more sharply to the left. At this time, however, he fell gravely ill and the question of his succession became acute.

The army leaders were deeply worried by the fear that Sukarno's left-wing advisers might maneuver themselves, during the course of his illness or death, into a position where they could seize the instruments of state power and set in motion a purge of the armed forces, eliminating those opposed to Communist party control. Similarly the left-wing leaders were worried lest the army leaders attempt a military coup on the same grounds of Sukarno's incapacity. It is clear that the top leadership of each group was secretly planning some type of counteraction in the event the other side moved decisively past a critical line (though it appears that neither side had defined for itself what that critical line might be). Possibly some first strike was being planned as well; at least, that is what each side accused the other of after the event.

It is certain that in Djakarta, on the night of September 30, 1965, bands of men in military uniforms set out to capture a number of the top army officers, killing some and missing others (and in one case killing the teen-age daughter of a general who escaped). It is also certain that Colonel Untung, an army man known for his left-wing sympathies, acknowledged himself the leader of that action and set up a movement among the junior military to continue the purge of high-ranking army officers. Accusing the generals of corruption and of treachery to Sukarno, he called on the public for moral support of his effort. It is certain too that the Communist party press published strong editorial approval of Untung's course, describing it, though, as an internal army matter that by implication did not justify more active external support. In the end the generals who had escaped, along with others, were able to rally army units and take quick counteraction; Colonel Untung and his followers retreated from Djakarta and were eventually captured. A few junior left-wing officers attempted to purge the senior military in other parts of Java, but their efforts, poorly coordinated and clumsily carried out, were swiftly put down.

The military leaders who extinguished the revolt took control of the government, arrested Sukarno's left-wing advisers, and set up trials to convict them and numerous other left-wing persons in and out of the armed forces of instigating the assassinations as part of a general plot. They privately implicated President Sukarno as well, and his political position was finally undermined to the point where he was driven into retirement. To what extent the Communist party and the left wing generally were directly responsible for the purges is unclear. It may be that, as in 1948, their hand was forced against their will by hotheaded action on the part of young left-wing officers.

What happened after that is very clear, however. An enormous wave of lynchings of persons with left-wing sympathies ripped through Java and other parts of Indonesia, carried out in part by local military units but much more massively by ordinary civilians. The massacre was tolerated and even encouraged by the army and the national police. According to available firsthand reports, a prominent role was played by groups of orthodox youths, many of them students from rural Muslim boarding schools sent out with the blessing and protective powers of their religious teachers. Orthodox communities rose up to attack suspected left-wing families in adjacent communities, and lynching bands roamed widely through the countryside, killing at will.

Virtually no organized resistance was raised against them, not even by the Communist party. Earlier, during the dispute with the Netherlands over New Guinea and especially during the confrontation with Malaysia, the Communists had pressed hard for the training and arming of a people's militia, which they might hope to control. But for that very reason the army had always successfully opposed the creation of a militia, and the left wing never regained any of the military and paramilitary organization it lost at Madiun. Moreover the steady progovernment stance taken by the Communist party and its affiliates as part of their alliance with Sukarno, as well as the extremely bureaucratic character of their organizations, left their members poorly prepared for a rush to the barricades. The bands of lynchers were easily able to wreak vengeance on whomever they chose to attack.

So much for a historical view. The strand of process I have been distinguishing — the growth of and the change in the religious and cultural antithesis between Islamic orthodoxy and Javanese syncretism — plainly connects the 1965 massacres with a long train of historical events. That process, as I stated earlier, is denied any special causal standing in any of those events, but it does yield some sense of future possibilities in Java and lights up events in the past. It helps "explain" the massacres in a certain intellectual sense, much as a murder story explains a murder.

I now turn to the second part of my essay, a view of the event as a form of personal experience, using for the purpose a particular account of events during the Madiun Affair in 1948 (none was yet available for the massacres of 1965). The account is translated from a short novel by Pramudya Ananta Tur, probably the outstanding Indonesian writer of the postwar period, who, incidentally, was reported missing during the 1965 massacres. The novel, *Dia Jang Menjerah* ("One Who Gave Up"),[4] is set in Blora, the central Javanese town that was Tur's home. Jailed by the Dutch in Djakarta at the time of the Madiun Affair, Tur returned to Blora after his release, and his description of events there comes from the firsthand accounts of friends and relatives.

The novel concerns a family of the town whose father is a pro-Republican official. The family has its own history: the mother has died a few years before the story begins; there are eight children, two boys in their early twenties, three teen-age sisters, and three younger children. The two older boys have gone off as volunteer laborers to Burma during the Japanese occupation and not returned (volunteer work from which, because of the hardships, not many came back). The eldest daughter has a close but tense relationship with the father, whose authority she resents. He is a committed Indonesian nationalist, intensely loyal to the established Republic, who views any radicalism as a threat to the new state. She is strongly drawn toward left-wing radicalism, and when the left-wing partisans take power in Blora, she goes off with a Communist cavalry troop. The father has a stroke in consequence.

Shortly after, while he is still ill, the Communists arrest him and put him in jail.

A neighboring couple move into the house, uninvited, ostensibly out of pity to care for the remaining children, but in fact to steal whatever they can. The children dare make no protest. There is a sense of terror all around them as informers become active, and opportunists and sadists turn partisan in order to attack their neighbors and fellow workers.

The cavalry troop the oldest daughter has joined descends upon the home, the leader ordering the two teen-age sisters to join: "Turn Red or be treated as fowl" (which are readily slaughtered for meat or cash). The girls manage to persuade the leader to take only one of them. The older one sacrifices herself and is almost literally pulled from the arms of her sister.

I begin my translation at the point when the Republican troops drive out the Communist partisans and reoccupy the town. Diah, the remaining teen-age sister, has been further dazed by the horror of seeing a Red collaborator hunted down and killed in her own yard.

Suddenly a voice wailed out:
"The jail, the Reds are burning the jail!"
The cry was followed by the scream of a young woman:
"My husband, he's still in there, what will happen to him?"
The scream died.
Diah leaped up and ran out of the house. In her breast was only one thought: Father. Perhaps her father was in that jail. She ran and ran, straight toward the north, toward the jail, side by side with crowds of people whose relatives had been put in jail by the Reds. . . . Unused to running, she stopped from time to time to catch her breath. On the way she came upon a band of Republican soldiers holding prisoner a young boy whose clothes were in rags. On his head he still wore a red bandanna [an emblem of the Communist partisans].
"Red? Red?" asked the soldiers. "Red? Red?" shouted the soldiers at him. The youth finally just nodded his head. A soldier kicked him in the leg so that he fell to the ground. And again he was asked "Red?" The youth answered slowly. He was still lying sprawled in the dirt, face down. His feet were bare. "Yes." Then the youth was shot in the head. He spoke no more. He was grabbed by the feet and thrown into a truck. The truck

161

drove off. Gone. The girl, Diah, began crying. She covered up the blood of the victim with the dust of the road, and she ran and ran and ran. . . .

Hundreds of people stood outside the jail watching the soldiers carrying out the bodies of the victims. Close by Diah a woman ran one way and the other, hands crossed behind her back. Her son, a student at Gadjah Mada University, was also in jail and not yet saved. Diah gathered her strength and cried out at the top of her lungs, "Father . . . Father . . . Diah is here . . . Your child is here!" At that moment, the front gate of the jail was broken open from the outside. Another body was brought out. Two. Three. Bodies of men already crushed. People were murmuring behind her, "No, not him, not him." Suddenly someone from behind stooped and hugged one of those broken bodies. Another corpse was brought out. There remained only a piece of the trunk. After that a foot was thrown out. Diah shrieked "Father, Father." The foot had been crippled. Perhaps as a child its owner had stuck it on a stake. And that was the foot of her father, and the father of her brothers and sisters, and she cried out again "O Father." She cradled the foot. And covered its toes with her kisses. She started to run off with the foot, but a soldier stopped her. "Don't run off with that foot. Let's try to find the rest of the body. Don't run away with it." She stopped, confused, then indeed put it back in its place. Before putting it down, carefully, she kissed and kissed the toes all covered with blood, then bowed before it, over and over, honoring it. And then she ran straight as a mad person in at the front gate of the jail.

Others were crowding in, too, crying out for brothers, fathers, and sons. They entered every empty cell. The flames of the fire burned them and the smoke of the fire choked them. Bodies cut in pieces lay strewn about. Suddenly someone shouted not far away, "The well here is full of bodies." Those searching for someone not yet found ran to the edge of the well and stared down into it. Within they were looking at corpses of men. The water was red and in continual motion, for there were those down in it still alive. Soldiers ran back and forth, busy breaking open locked cells. Diah ran off calling out into each locked cell, but no one she knew was there. Sometimes there were only moans or coughs, because those were the ones who had been shot from outside before the Reds were beaten. Suddenly, a great gust of smoke arose, filled with dust and heat. A soldier grabbed Diah and pulled her out of the jail. People outside wept and wailed, and among the wails could be heard ringing out from time to time, "Here's a Red spy." Soldiers ran to catch the one pointed out. And shot him through the head. The walls of the jail collapsed. The crowds began to break up, going homeward weeping. Diah ran to find her father's foot, but the foot was gone.

As I have mentioned earlier, pale reflections of the events at Madiun appeared in the area where I did my fieldwork. In 1948 restraining factors were at work — the intervention of the Republican government and a sense of solidarity brought about by the war for independence. In 1965, on the other hand, there were no such protective influences — quite the contrary. Ideological and communal bitterness ran unchecked, tearing apart the delicate, often covert living patterns which groups and persons on each side of the schism had worked out to avoid abrasive touch with one another. In my area during 1953 and 1954 these techniques of avoidance worked to reduce interpersonal friction, but they contributed nothing toward building mutual support and concern among neighboring communities in the event of violence. Instead hostility and an urge to act violently grew in intensity, to the point that whenever I traveled from one area to another, I was eagerly seized on as a source of information about other communities, and my questioners always wanted the worst news they could hear. Though I have had no information about what happened in 1965 and 1966 in my village, I can extrapolate from the past and the result is horrible. Reportedly entire families were destroyed in great number, just as in Blora in 1948. I suspect that included among them were families who were kind and close to me during my stay and whose small affairs I knew well.

What was really destroyed in Blora was the very fabric of hope and trust by which a person is connected, through expanding rings of community, to parents and children, friends, neighbors, countrymen, and indeed all men. At the end of the story Ananta Tur's heroine Diah has become the title of the book, "One who gave up." The hope and trust through which she tried to reach some position of delicacy, of human sensitivity toward her world, have been smashed by the violence worked out in those around her — father, brothers, sisters, neighbors, strangers, the soldiers of the nation. She simply gives up, cutting off her sensitivity to any suffering, to hope, to value, as a person in extreme pain loses all sense of connection to the part that hurts.

It seems to me that the process of producing such total anomie must certainly have been greatly accelerated in Indonesia during and since the massacres. No doubt the same things are happening in other places for which Americans must feel most directly responsible. I make this point here as clearly as I can, because it seems to me that this view of the event in Indonesia in terms of particular personal experience reveals what most analyses of political events avoid revealing. Certainly my historical analysis, however satisfying, fails to reveal it. The destruction and unbelievable suffering that grind away a person's own values, that drive him to disconnect his self from even his own immediate world, are thought to be of too little consequence to merit weighing in contributions to scholarship or to policy. The little circle of consequence surrounding one person's destruction, or one family's destruction, is too tiny to count. And five hundred thousand times zero is of course still zero.

REFERENCES

1. Most references have been omitted for purposes of economy. They may be found in my monograph *Religion and Politics in Rural Central Java*, Yale University Southeast Asia Studies, Cultural Report Series no. 12 (1963).

2. For a detailed description of their character, see Sartono Kartodirdjo, *The Peasants' Revolt of Banten in 1888*, Verhandelingen van het Koninklijk Instituut voor Taal-, Land- en Volkenkunde, vol. 50 (The Hague: Martinus Nijhoff, 1966).

3. Smail, *Bandung in the Early Revolution*, Cornell University Southeast Asia Program, Modern Indonesia Project Monograph Series (1964).

4. Djakarta: Pustaka Rakjat N.V., 1950.

Index

Index

167